Killer Technique®: Flatpicking Guitar

by Colin Botts and Corey Christiansen

1 2

Visit us on the Web at www.melbay.com — E-mail us at email@melbay.com

Table of Contents

Introduction

Having good, efficient technique is paramount in becoming a great guitarist. By improving technique, a guitarist can do more by working less. Many of the exercises in this book are very basic and may seem simple at first, but they get harder. Also, playing even the easiest exercises perfectly can be challenging for an experienced guitarist. The idea is to take these workouts slowly. By doing so, proper technique will be acquired and hand injury will be avoided.

Synchronizing the right and left hand is a constant battle. If it were easy, everybody would be able to play the guitar at a high level. Many guitarists have found success in building technique by working the right and left hand separately. If a new technique is being worked on for developing the right hand, make the exercise easy for the left in the beginning. If a technique is being worked on for left-hand development, make it relatively easy for the right hand. As the level of technique for both the right and left hand increases, what used to be hard will become easy for both hands. Each guitarist should use these exercises as a springboard to create workouts of their own, a process which can be never-ending. The trick is to find a methodical way to create these workouts and stay organized.

Chromatic Exercises

Having independence between each finger of the left hand will help guitarists execute passages that are not necessarily "guitar friendly." These next exercises will help achieve left-hand finger independence. The patterns below are based on four-note chromatic lines that can be played on all six strings. Each student should use these fingerings on all six strings and in other positions of the fingerboard. Since the pattern makes use of the four fingers of the left hand, there are a total of 24 permutations (shown below the musical example) that can be derived and played on each string. Use one or two of the permutations a day (or week) as a warm up exercise. These exercises should be played with alternate picking.

Example 1: Fingering pattern 1-2-3-4

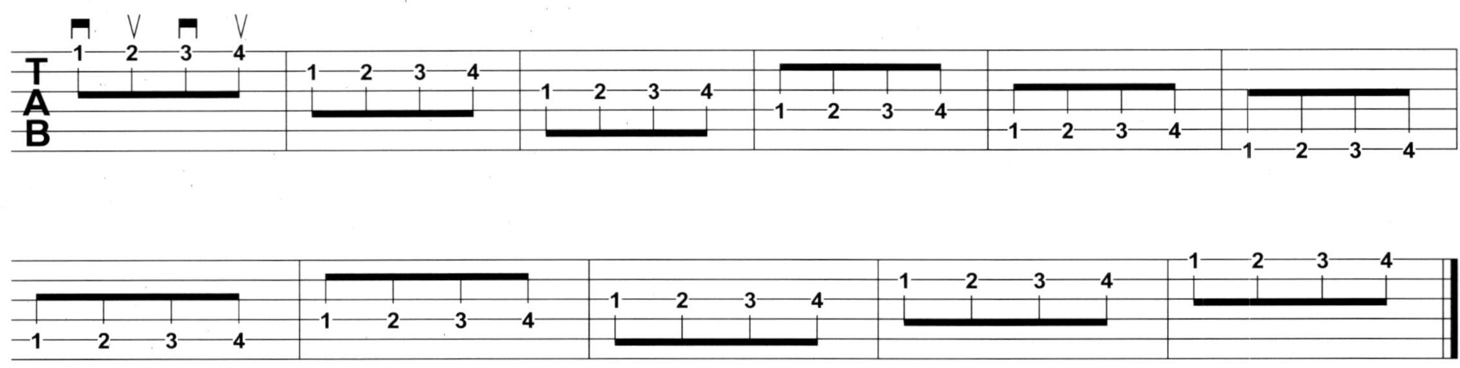

Example 2: Fingering pattern 1-2-4-3

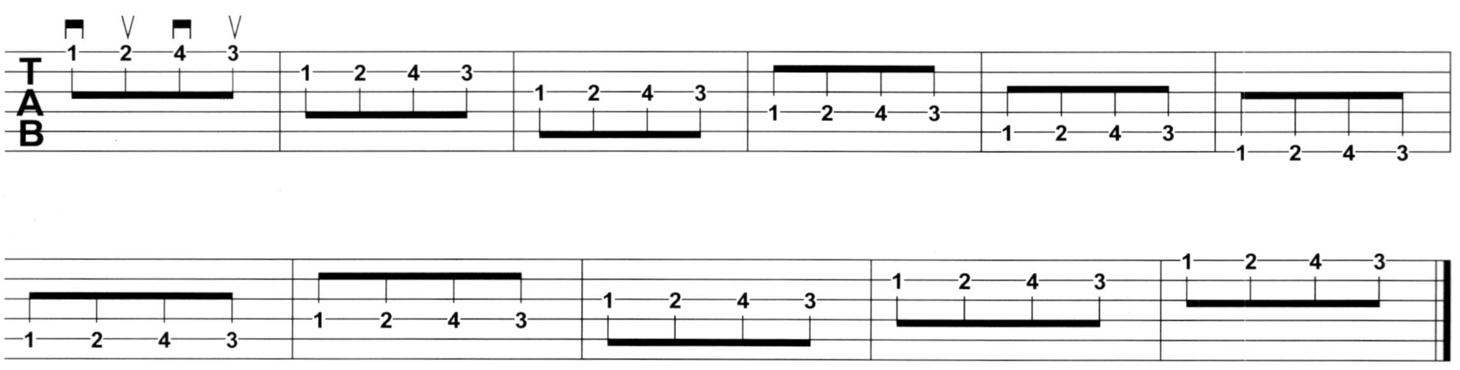

A complete list of 1234 permutations is shown below. Practice these to develop left-hand dexterity.

1234	2134	3124	4123
1243	2143	3142	4132
1324	2314	3214	4213
1342	2341	3241	4231
1423	2413	3412	4312
1432	2431	3421	4321

Finger Independence

If a weakness between two (or more) fingers is found, it is important to isolate those fingers and play patterns that will help develop the transition or execution between those fingers. The following examples will provide some ideas of ways to develop weak finger combinations. The next three examples start with the first finger.

Exercise 1: First and Second Fingers

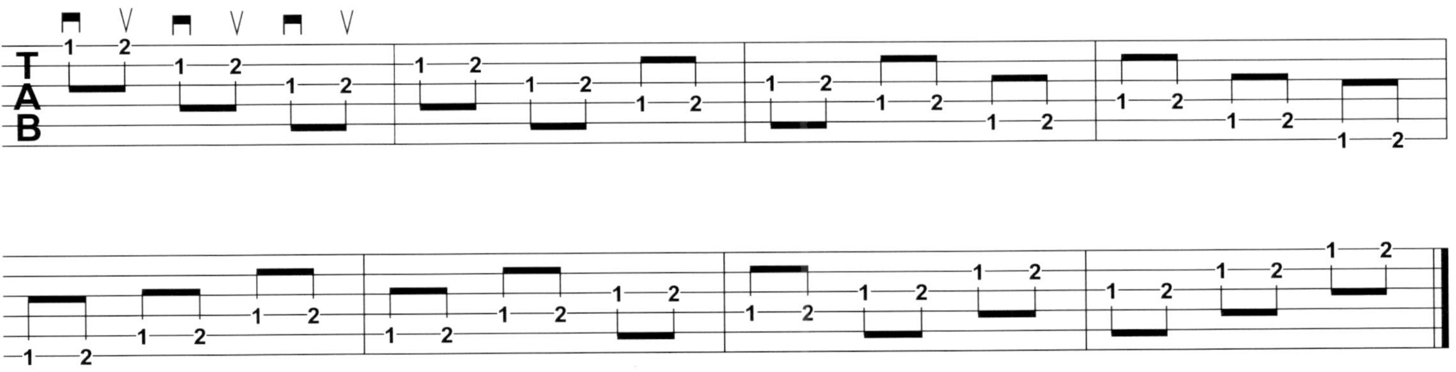

Exercise 2: First and Third Fingers

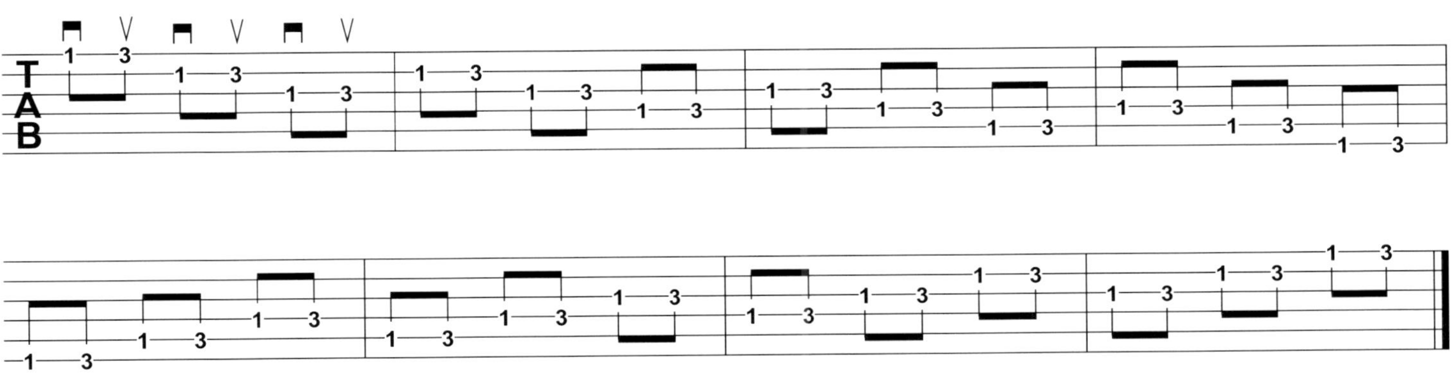

Exercise 3: First and Fourth Fingers

These three exercises all start with the second finger.

Exercise 4: Second and First Fingers

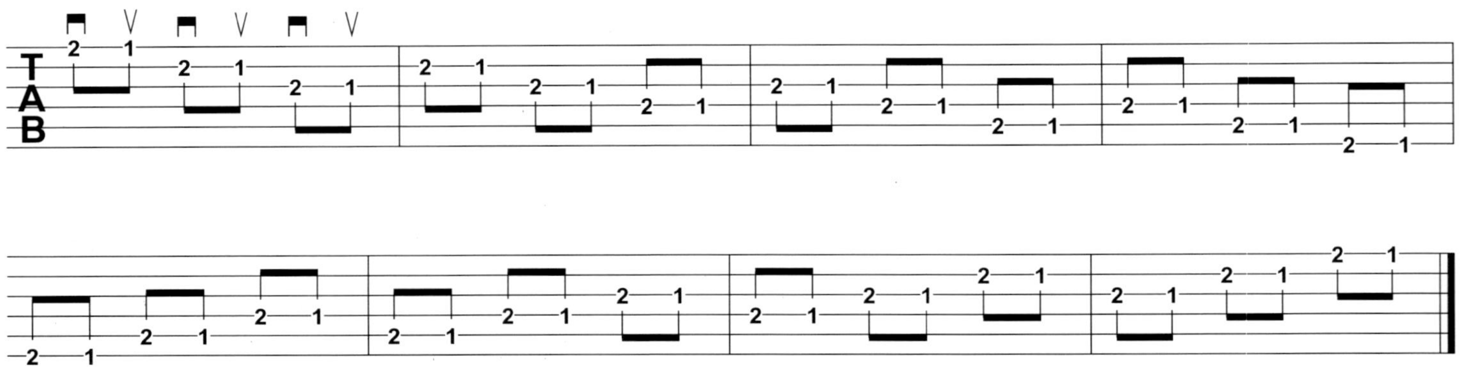

Exercise 5: Second and Third Fingers

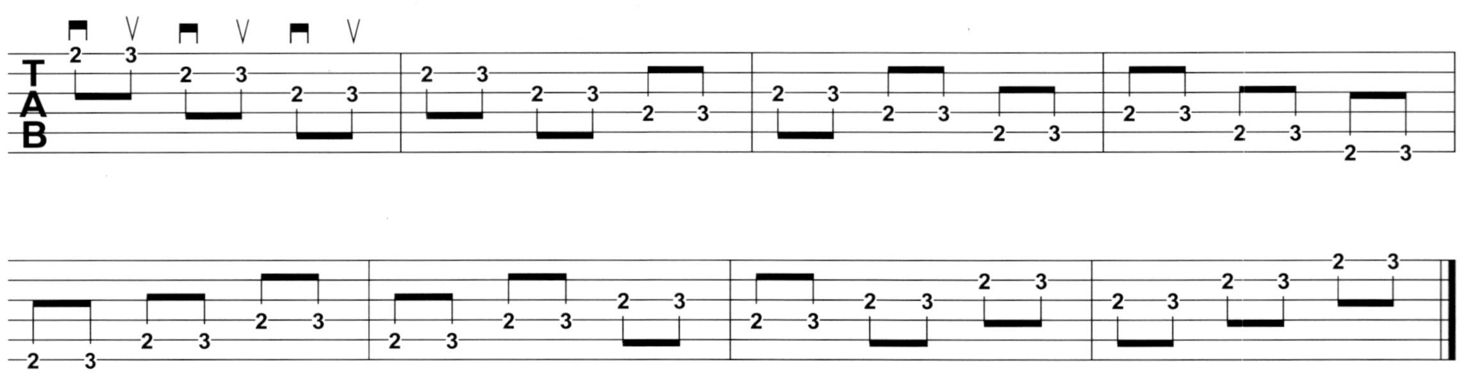

Exercise 6: Second and Fourth Fingers

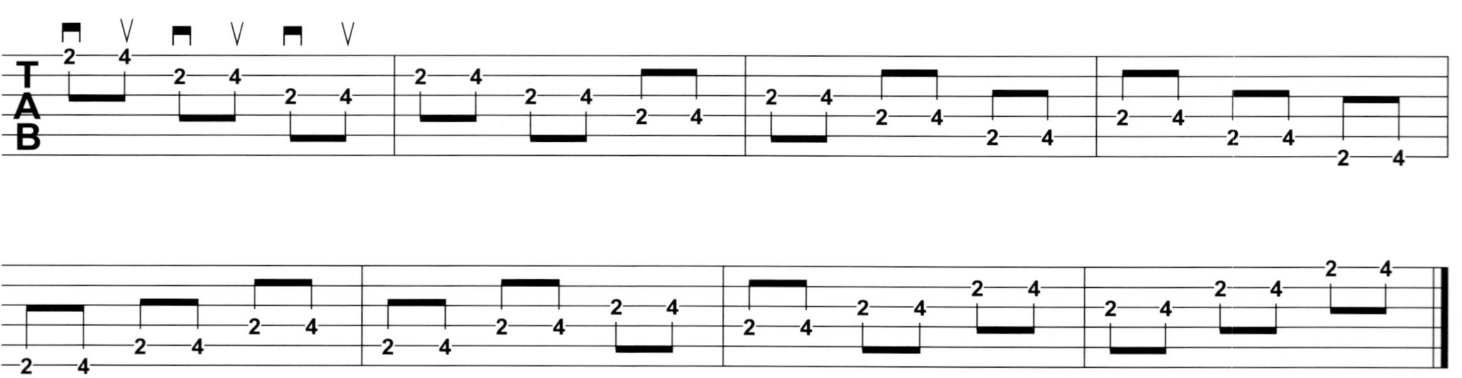

Each student should explore this type of exercises starting with each finger. You may also want to experiment with different string combinations as well as by playing each note twice as an eighth note, three times as triplets, and four times as sixteenth notes.

String Skipping

With a bit of practice most guitarists are able to pick multiple notes in succession on a single string. What proves much more challenging is accurately moving the pick from string to string. These next exercises provide an opportunity to isolate and practice picking different string combinations.

While there are various ways of picking these exercises, for purposes of consistency and gaining accuracy be sure to practice these using alternate picking. The exercises indicate only what string combinations are to be played.

Feel free to be creative and try holding various chord shapes with your left hand while working on these picking patterns. In order to isolate and practice individual string groups you may want to consider repeating each measure several times before moving onto the next one.

Skipping from the 6th String:

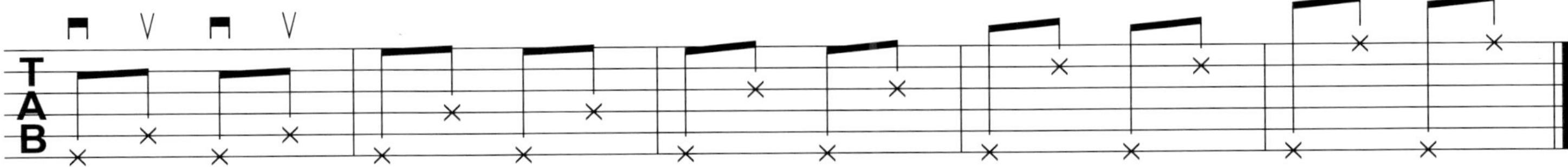

Skipping from the 5th String:

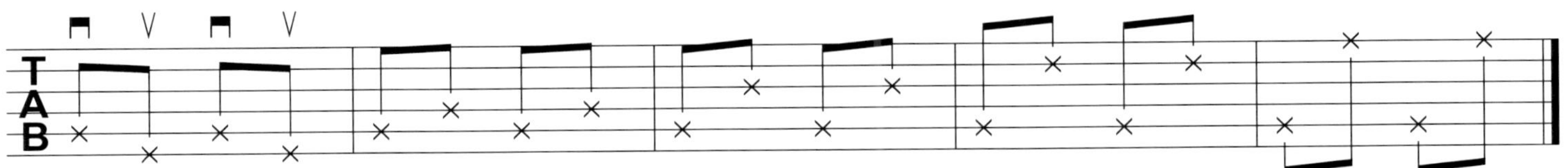

Skipping from the 4th String:

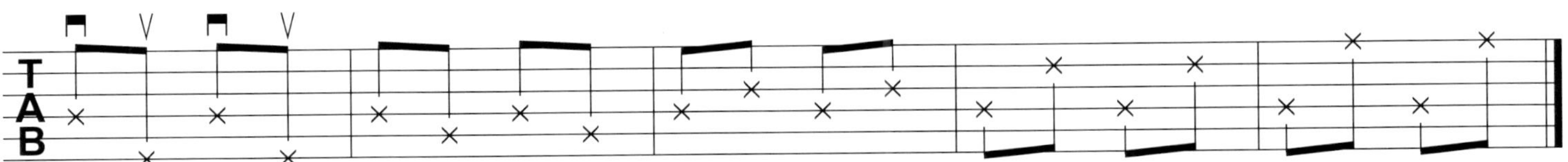

Skipping from the 3rd String:

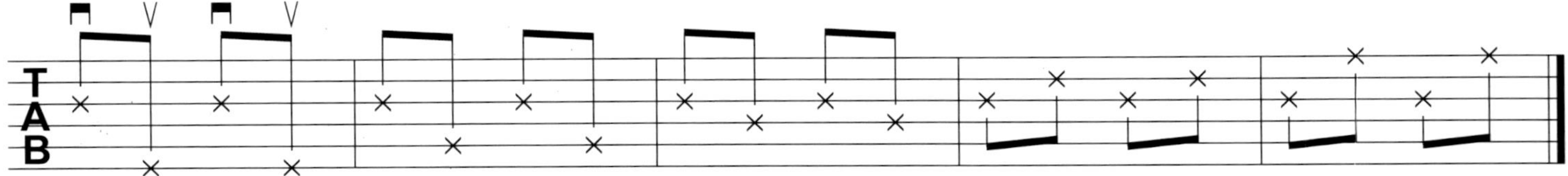

Skipping from the 2nd String:

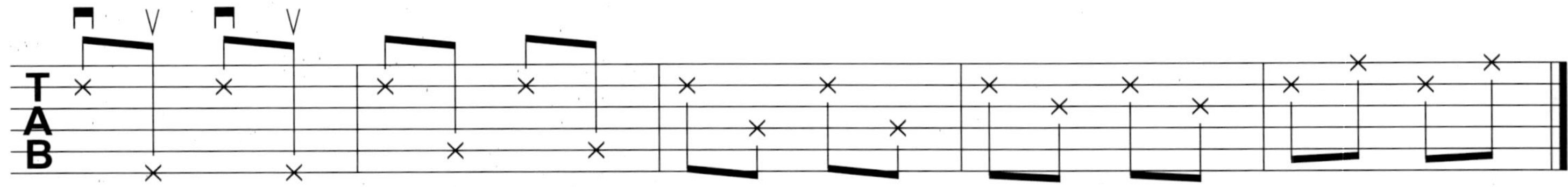

Skipping from the 1st String:

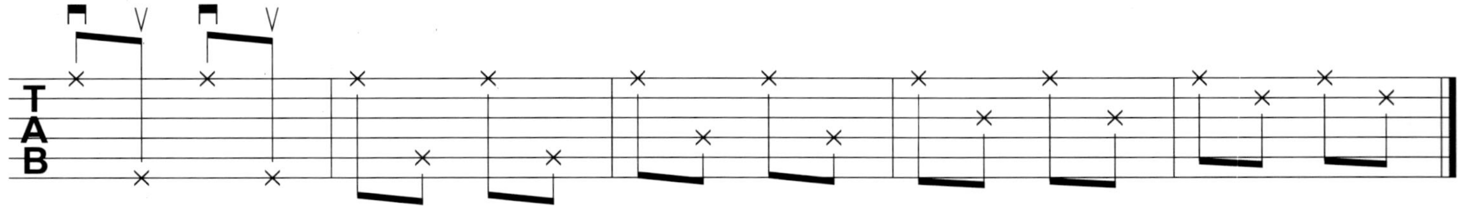

Experiment with the previous exercises by varying the number of times you play each string as demonstrated in the example below.

Skipping from the 6th String, Triplets:

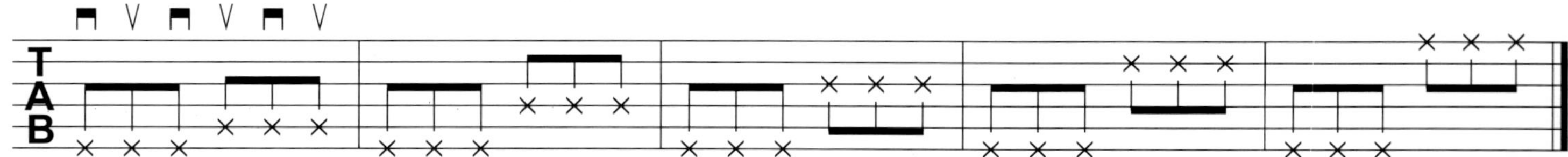

Tremolo

The next series of exercises are tremolo studies. Like the string skipping exercises presented earlier, tremolo exercises are a great way of working on picking accuracy. Use alternate picking when executing these exercises. This can be challenging, but the picking control that is gained is well worth the effort. Notice that while G major is used in all of the example exercises, they should be played in a variety of keys and positions on the guitar.

Tremolo #1:

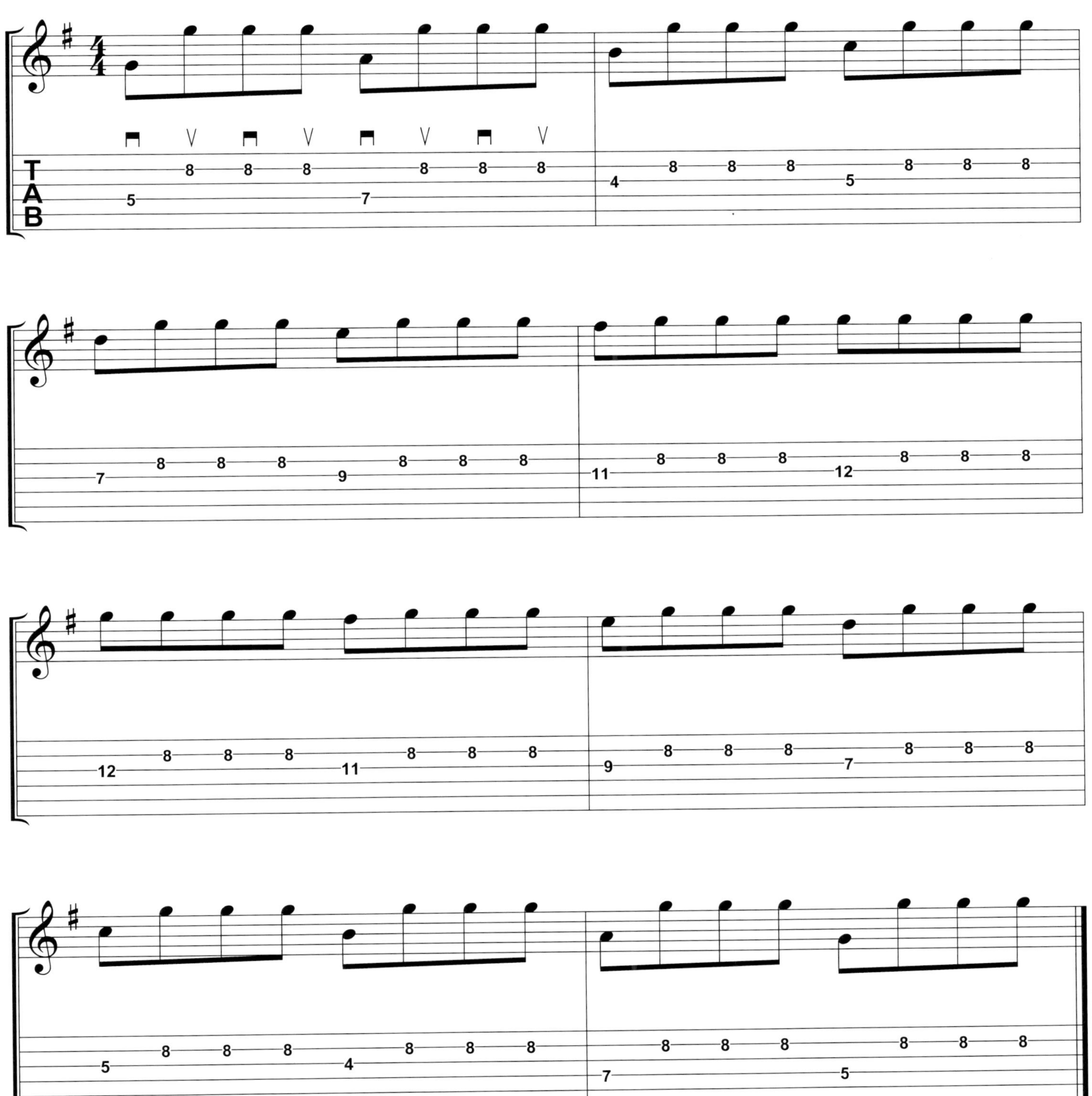

Tremolo #2:

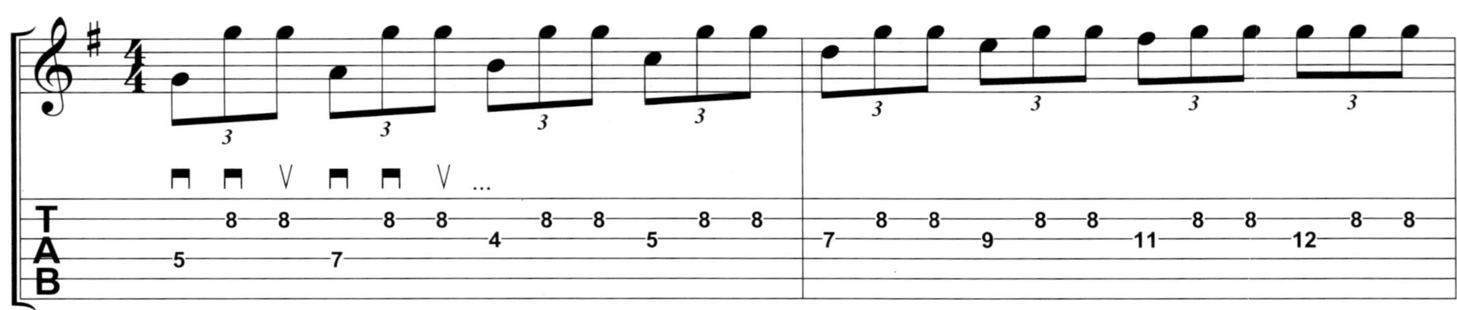

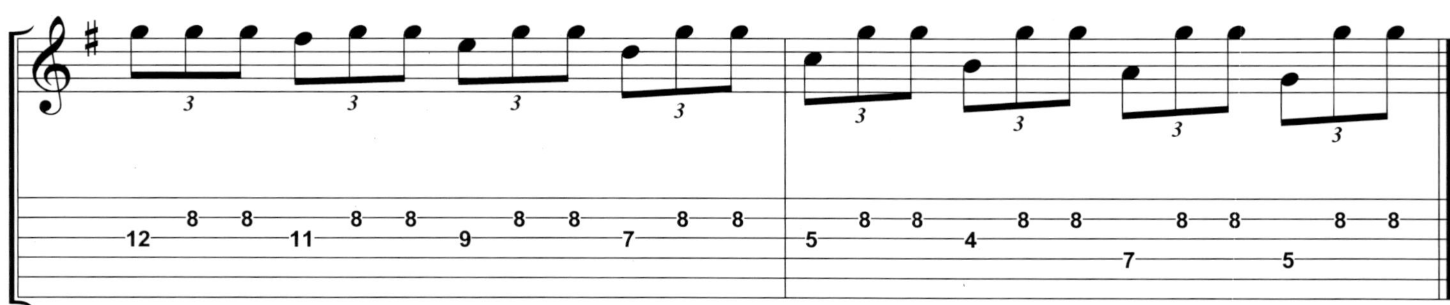

Tremolo #3:

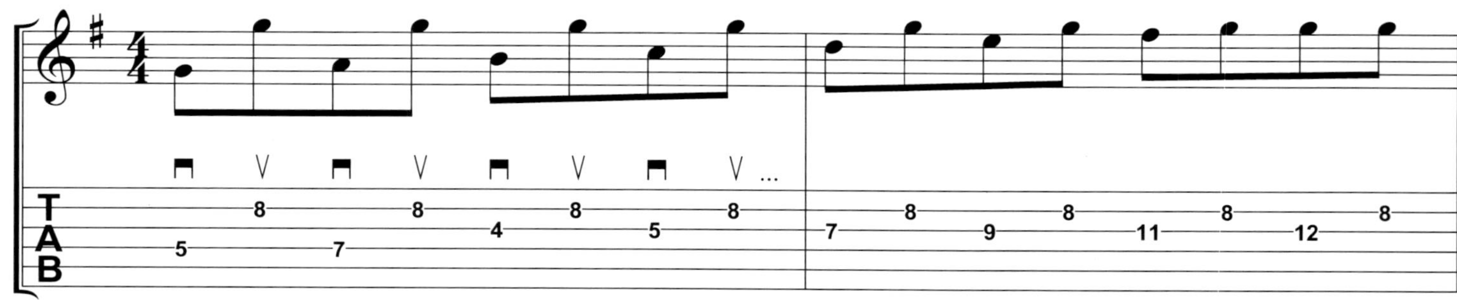

Scalar Patterns

There really isn't a substitute for using scales and scalar patterns to develop technique. The finger combinations are almost limitless when you figure that every scale type in every key, using a variety of fingerings, can be used. There are many other elements to playing great than just knowing scales, but they are important and can be used in a variety of ways to build technique.

There are many scalar patterns (or scalar sequences) that could be learned and practiced—so many we can't display even a fraction of them in this book. However, there are some easy techniques that can be used to develop scalar patterns. Most people have an easy time sequencing numbers; so to begin, assign every note in the scale (G major) a number. You may notice that the numbering for the example shown in the book corresponds to the scale degree. This doesn't need to be the case, it just worked out that way. Students can assign the number "1" to the highest note in the scale and number them backwards. It doesn't really matter.

G Major Scale

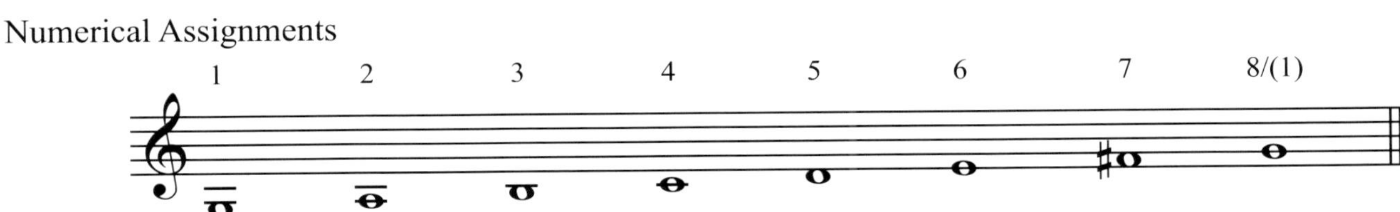

Next, sequence a pattern of numbers such as 1-2-3, 2-3-4, 4-5-6 etc. Then simply assign the right notes from the scale and play the patterns. Executing the patterns can be the challenging part. Remember that each sequence has an opposite or a reverse. 1-2-3, 2-3-4 would be 4-3-2, 3-2-1. It is important to use sequences in both directions.

The following examples demonstrate how this can be done. Be sure to do this type of exercise on different string groups, with different types of scales, and in a variety of keys.

Example 1: Scale Pattern 1-2-3, 2-3-4, 3-4-5 etc.

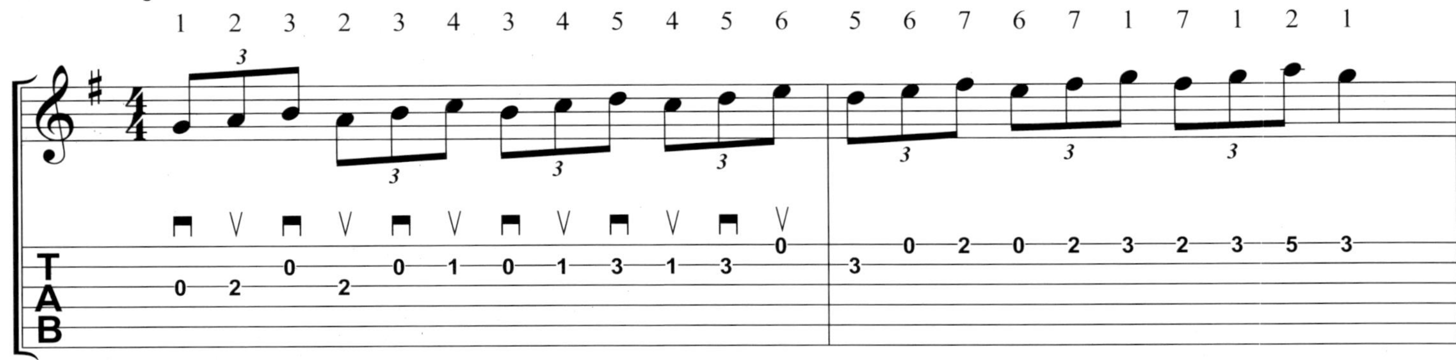

Example 2: Scale Pattern 1-7-1, 2-1-2, 3-2-3 etc.

Example 3: Scale Pattern 1-2-3-4, 2-3-4-5, 3-4-5-6 etc.

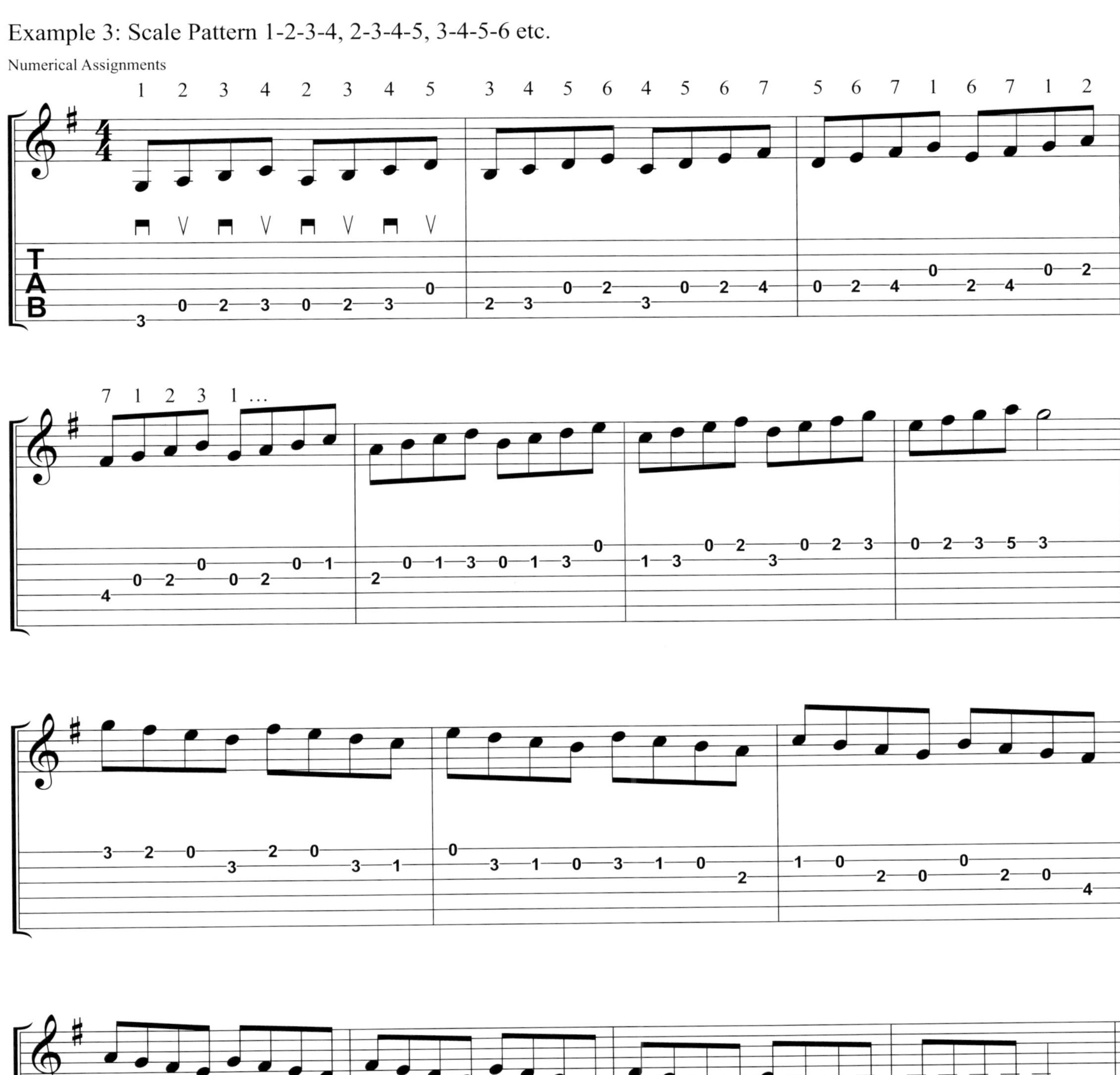

Open-String Shifting

In order to play higher up the neck it becomes necessary to shift your left hand position. Through the use of open-string shifting, guitarists are able to move fluidly up and down the guitar neck while avoiding awkward sliding or choppy sounding notes. To practice this technique, try playing a scale starting in first position. Upon reaching an open string, play that note and shift up the neck to the next note on the scale in another position on the neck.

For example, play a G major scale in first position. When you reach B on the open second string, rather than continuing on the second string with C on the first fret, try shifting up the neck and playing C on the fifth fret of the G string and continue up the scale in that position. Try practicing the examples outlined below. Be sure to practice scales in a variety of keys and positions.

Exercise 1: The following exercise requires you to shift from the open second string to fifth position, as illustrated below.

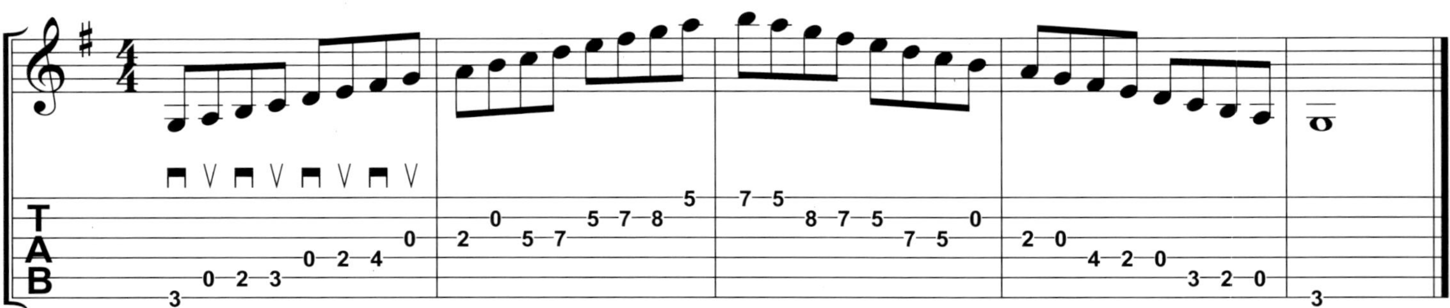

Exercise 2: The following exercise requires you to shift from the open first string to seventh position, as illustrated below.

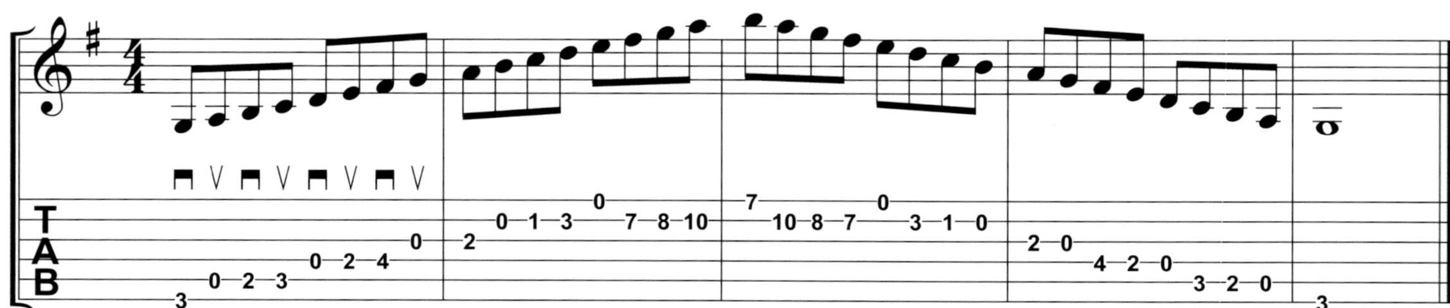

Exercise 3: The following exercise requires you to shift from the open third string to seventh position, as illustrated below.

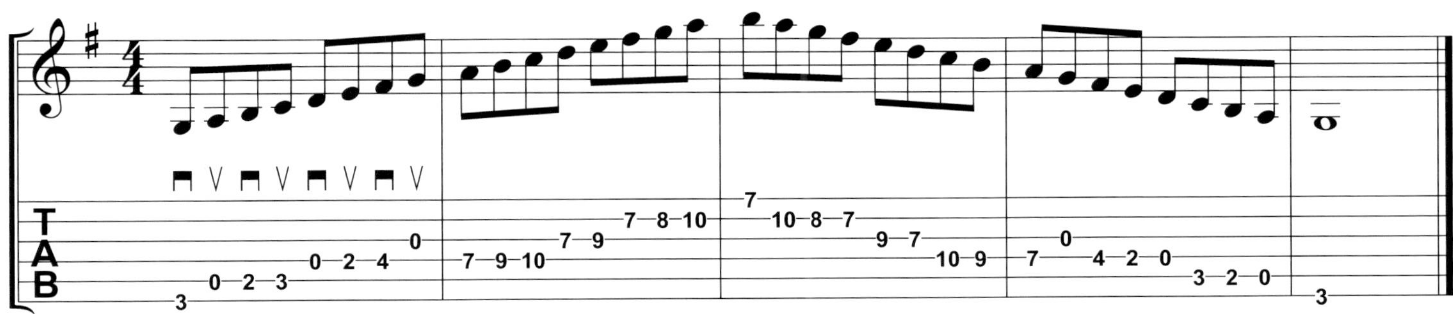

The previous exercises were all in the key of G. Here are a few examples of open string shifting on other scales. Be sure to explore other keys and shifting possibilities in order to expand your familiarity with the fingerboard.

Exercise 4: The following exercise is in the key of C. Shift from the open second string to fifth position.

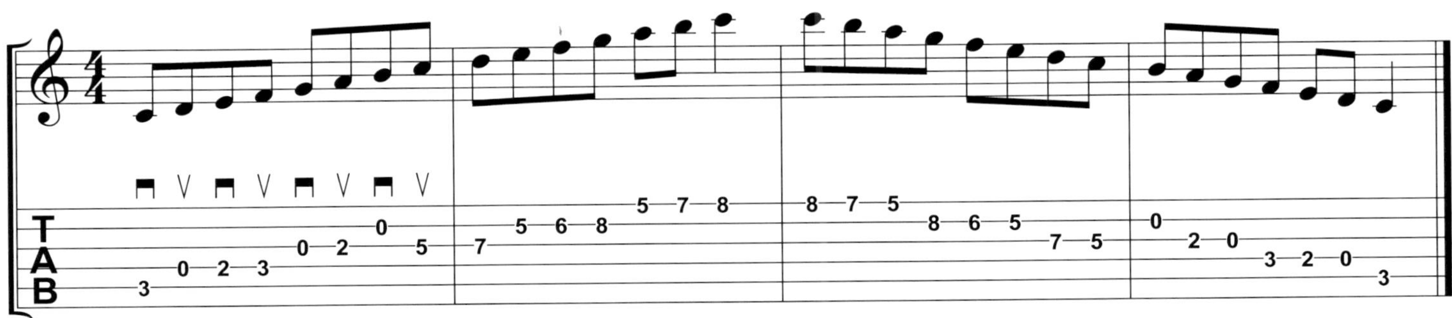

Exercise 5: This exercise is in the key of D. Shift from the open second string to seventh position.

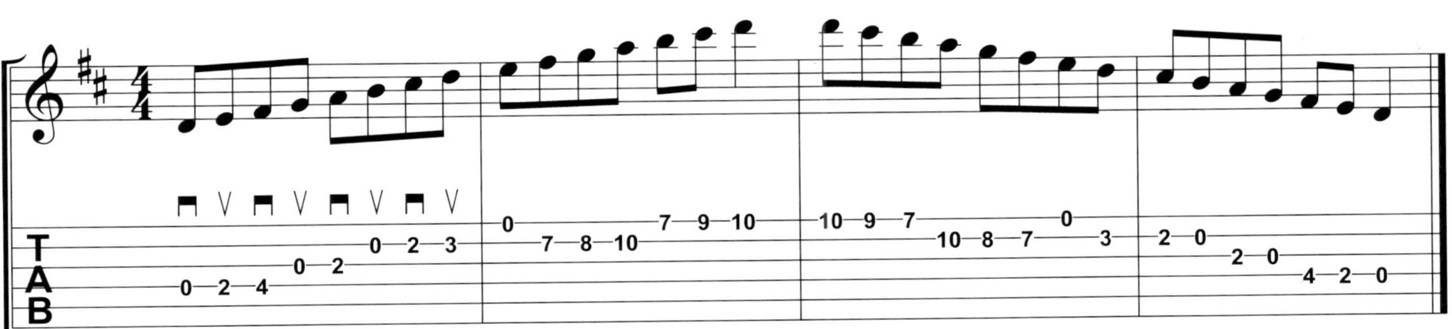

Exercise 6: This exercise is in the key of F. Shift from the open first string to tenth position.

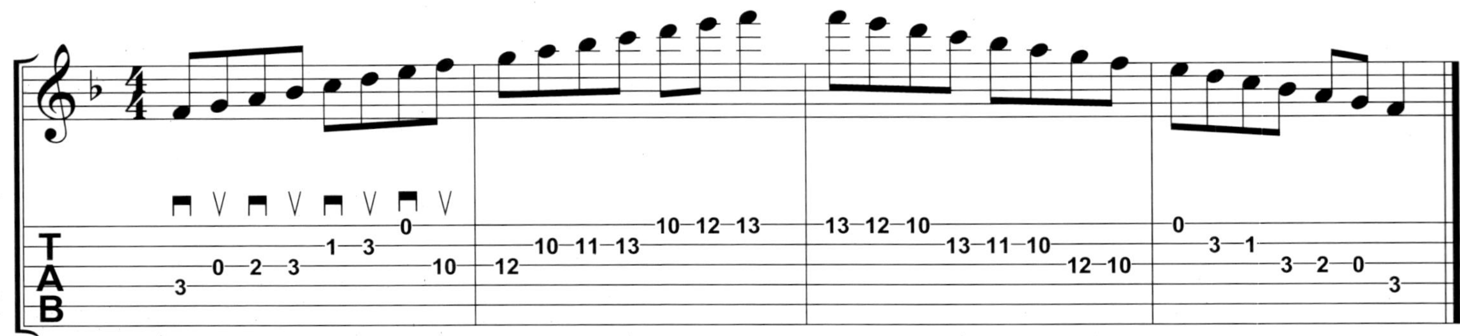

The technique of open string shifting can be applied to other more complex scale patterns and sequences, such as the next two examples. These exercises also utilize a right hand technique called *crosspicking* that will be covered in greater detail in the next section of this book.

Exercise 7: The following exercise ascends the G major scale in thirds and makes use of multiple open strings. (Notice the examples of crosspicking that occur in measures 3, 4, and 5.)

Exercise 8: The next exercise is a scale sequence in G that makes use of open string shifting and adjacent string combinations to achieve a fluid and legato sound. (This approach to playing is commonly used by bluegrass banjo players and is known as *melodic* style.)

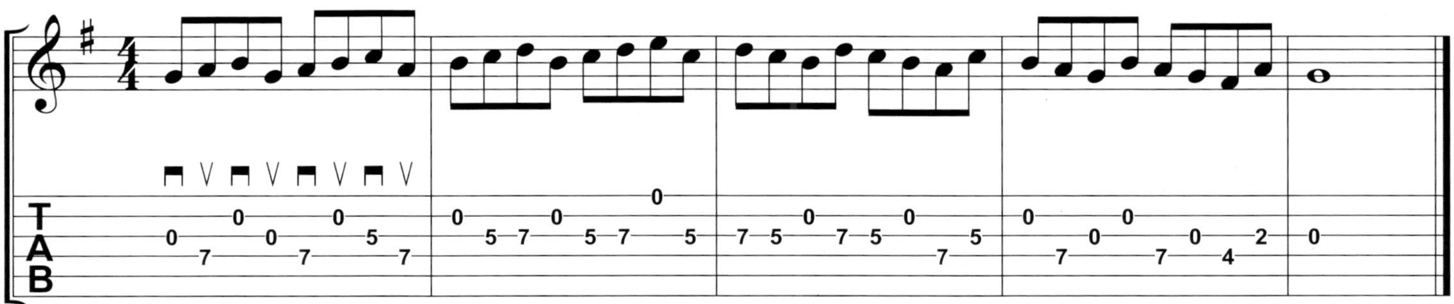

When practicing open string shifting on scales be sure to practice a variety of keys and types of scales. The last two exercises utilize open string shifting on pentatonic scales.

Exercise 9: G Major Pentatonic

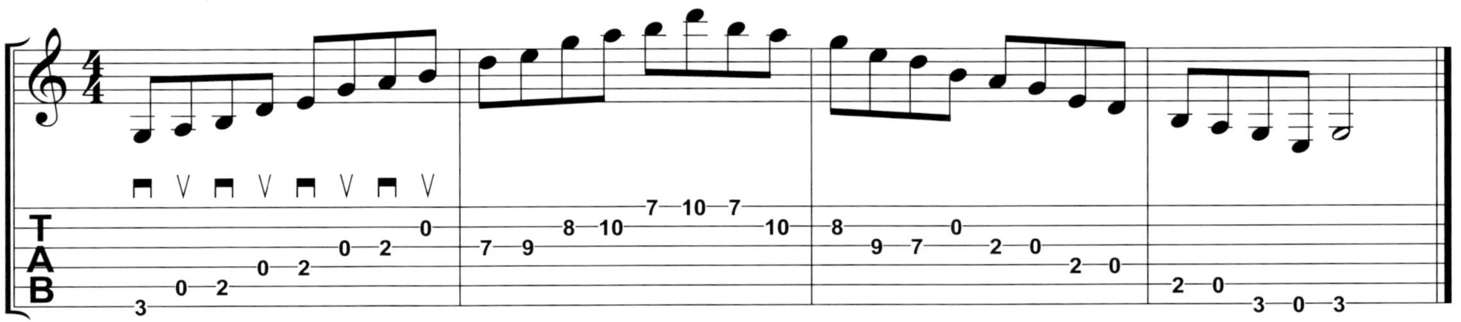

Exercise 10: C Major Pentatonic

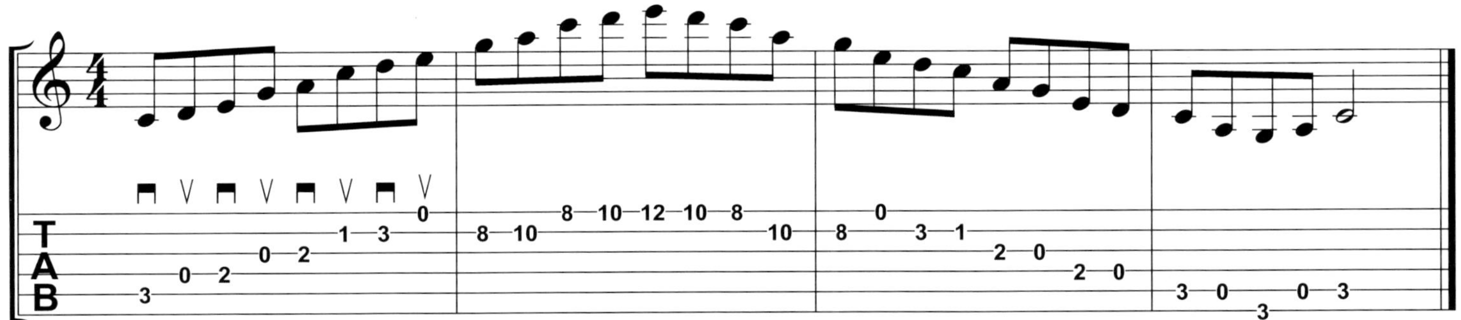

Now that you have learned these exercises, try creating your own scale patterns and other sequences in various keys and familiarize yourself with the many open string shifting possibilities that are available.

Lick Transposition

The best way to truly learn any style of music is to listen to great players of that style and learn their licks. This approach can be taken a step further—any such licks can be practiced in a variety of keys and positions on the guitar. Such practice will present technical challenges to overcome while at the same time being fun and musical.

The following examples are different flatpicking licks that have been transposed into a variety of keys. Notice the unique character of each key as well as the different technical challenges that result as you transpose the licks.

Lick #1

Key of F

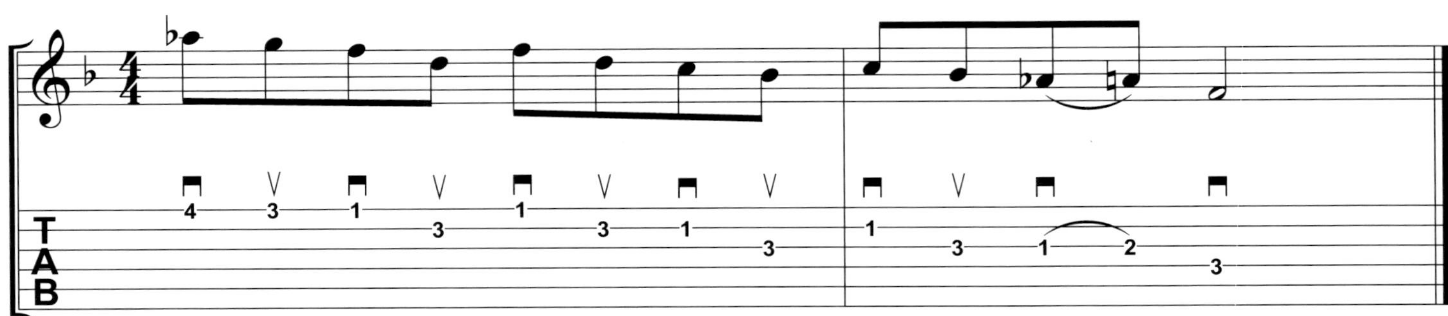

Key of C

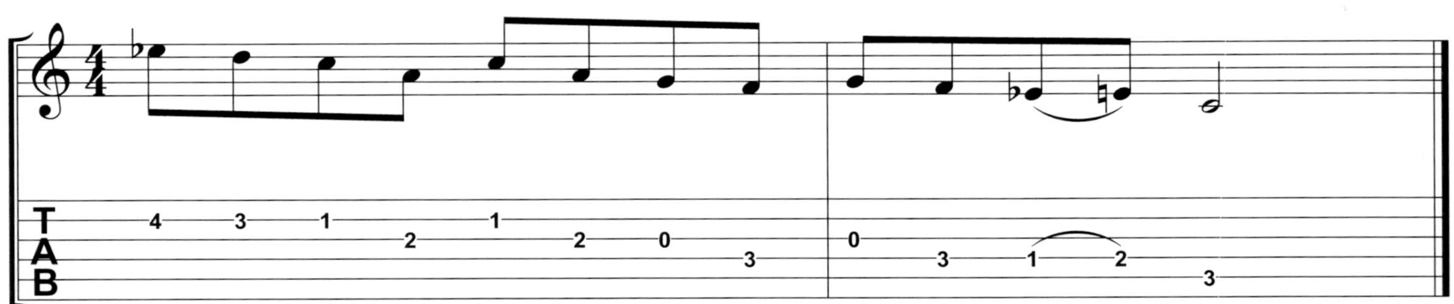

Key of G

Key of D

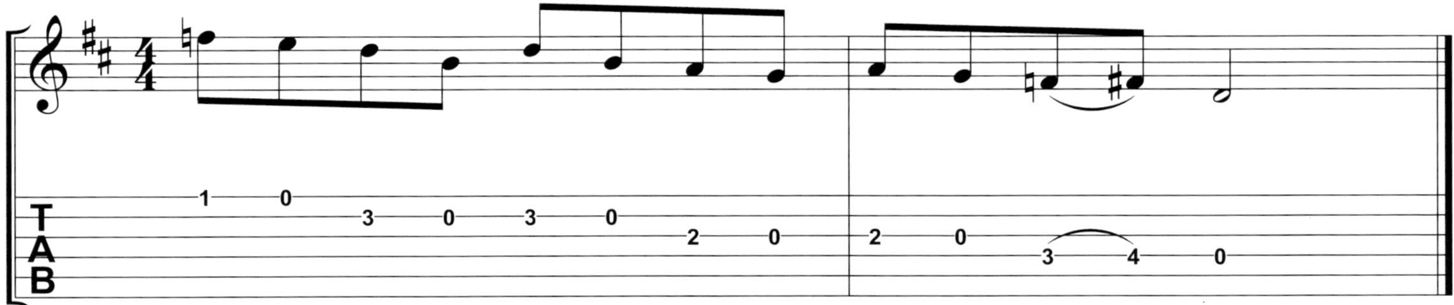

Key of A

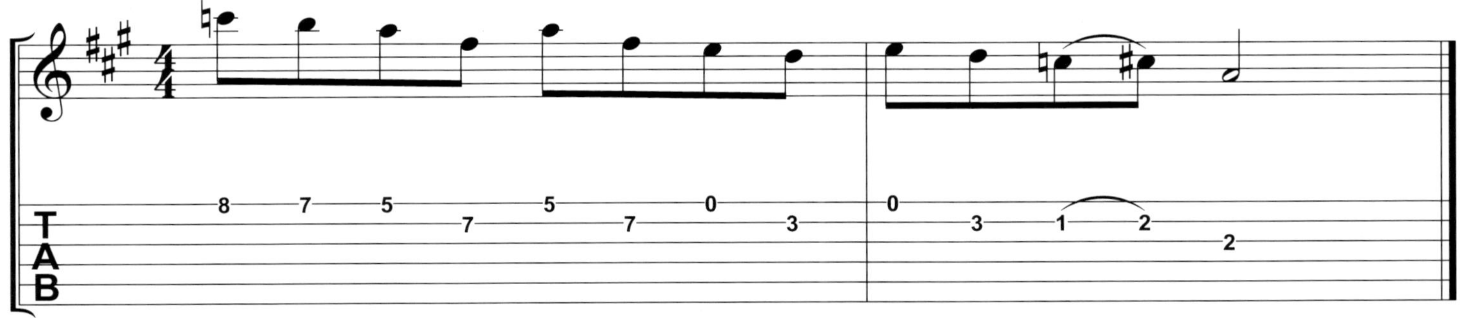

Key of E

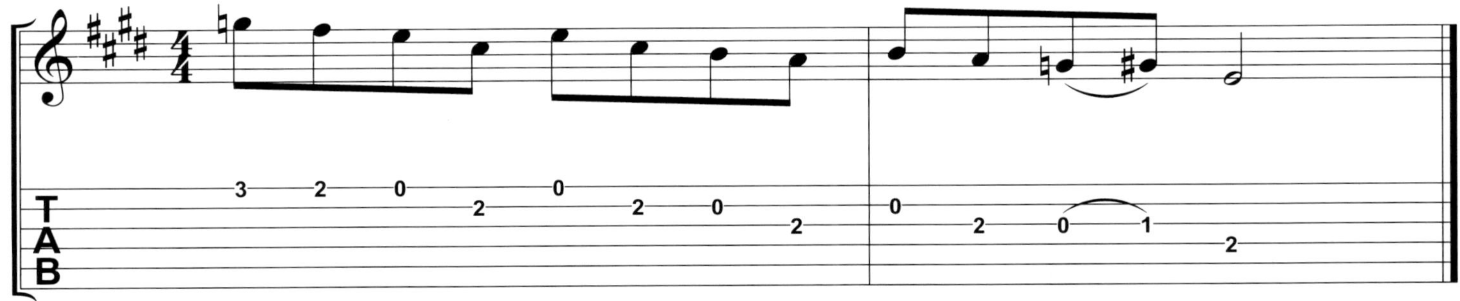

Lick #2

Key of F

Key of C

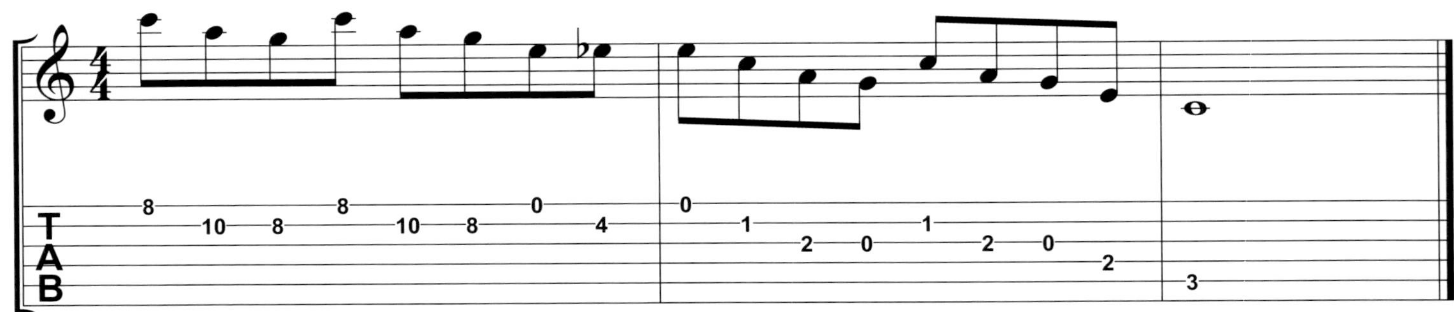

Key of G

Key of D

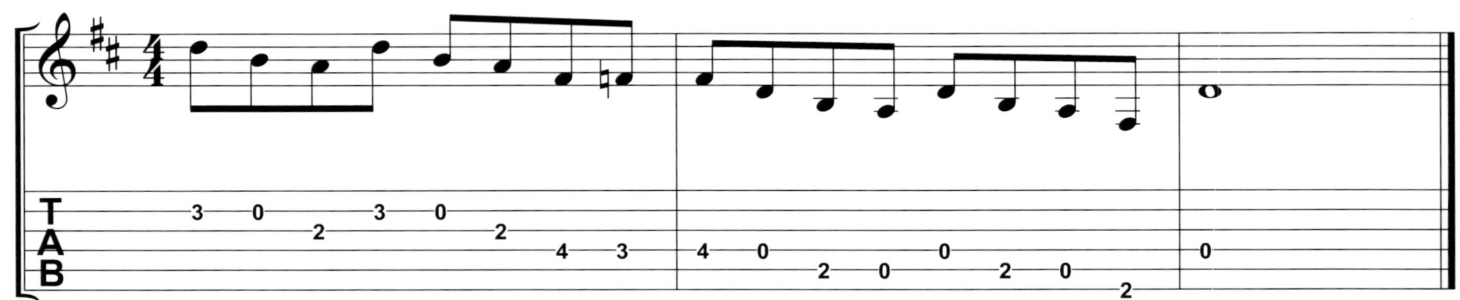

Key of A

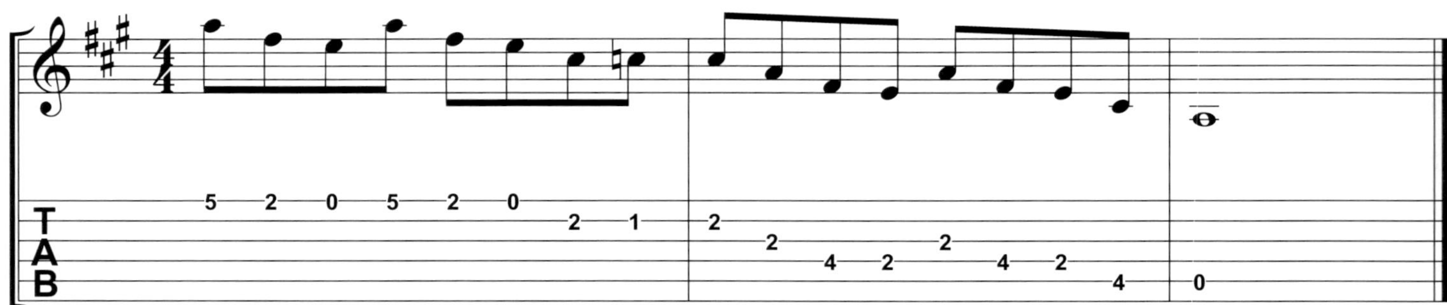

Key of E

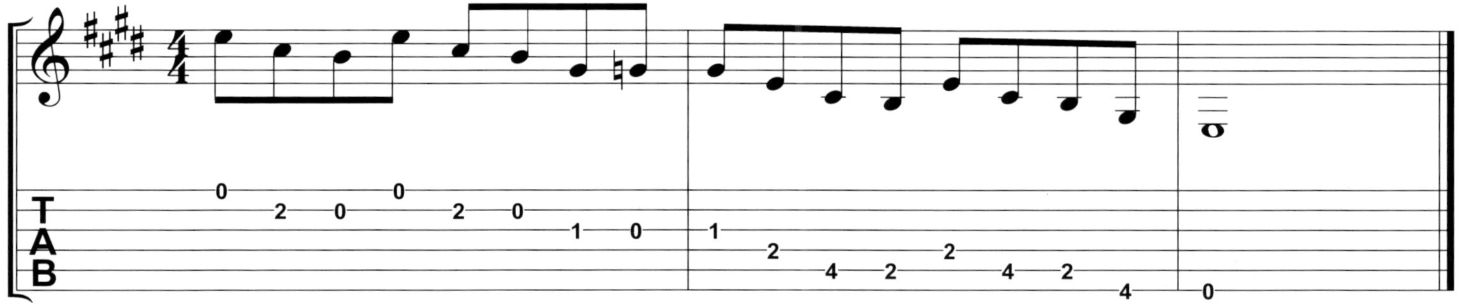

Lick #3

Key of F

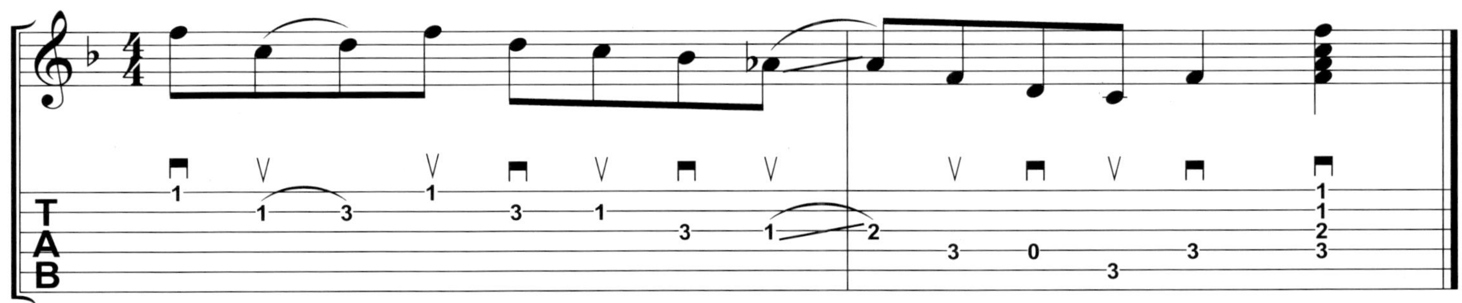

Key of C

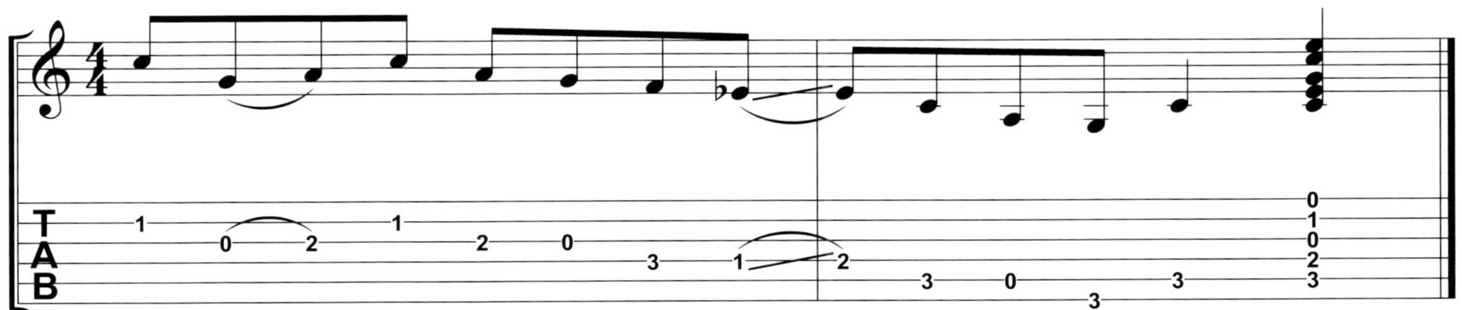

Key of G

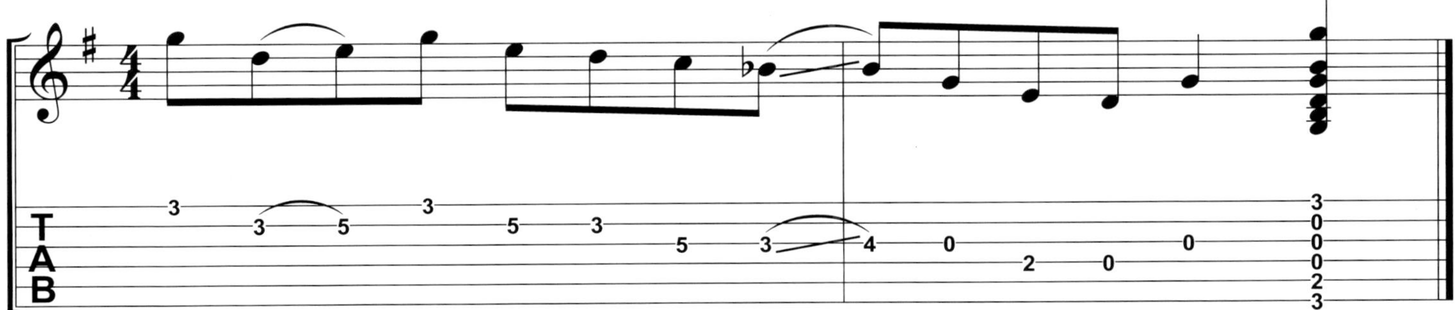

Key of D

Key of A

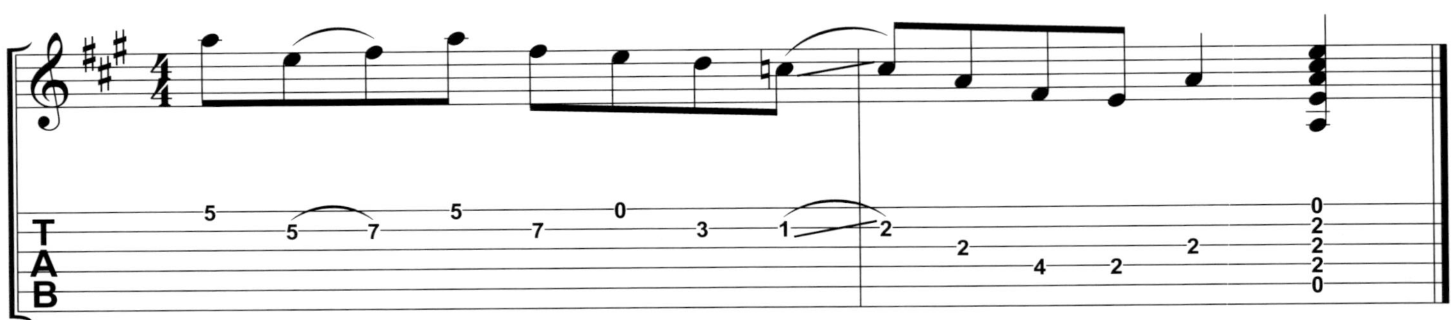

Key of E

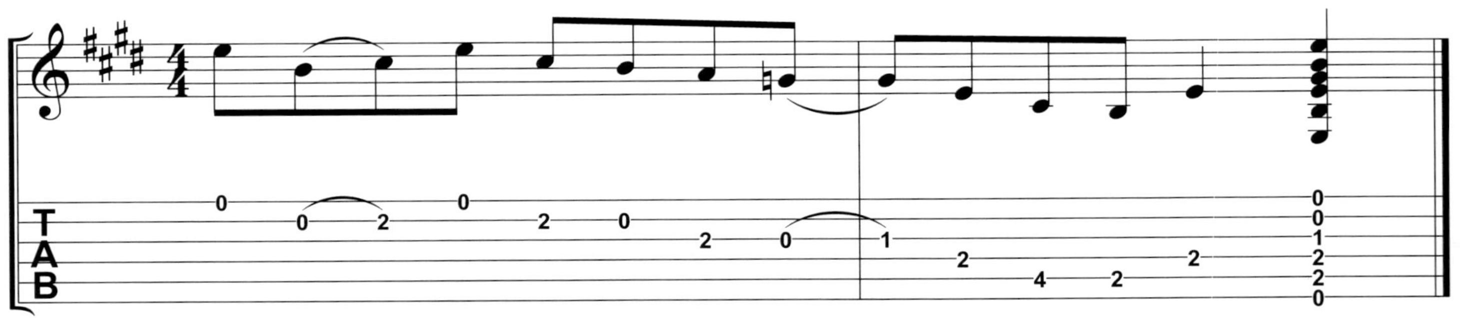

Now that you have worked through these different licks and transpositions, try taking some of your own favorite licks and learn them in a number of keys and positions.

Crosspicking

Crosspicking, a popular flatpicking guitar technique, poses certain challenges for the right hand. Crosspicking consists of playing a series of three or four-note arpeggios with the right hand. These repeating arpeggios, known as *rolls*, are often played on adjacent strings of the guitar while holding chord shapes with the left hand. As there are many possible roll patterns, only a few of the more popular ones will be covered in this book. You should familiarize yourself with the rolls presented below and then practice your own variations, experimenting with other string combinations and picking possibilities. All of the exercises below are played over a C chord. As you are experimenting with alternate string and pick combinations, be sure to include other chords.

In the first crosspicking exercise pictured below the right hand executes a three-note roll pattern, often called a *forward roll*. Strict alternate picking (down on the beat and up on the off-beat) is to be used regardless of what string is being played. As the pattern consists of an odd number of notes, the pick pattern is reversed every other time through the pattern (down up down, up down up).

Crosspicking #1: Forward Roll, Alternate Picking

The next crosspicking exercise, called a *reverse roll*, is also to be played using alternate picking. As in the above example, the odd number of notes in the sequence can present a challenge to the right hand, as the picking pattern reverses itself every other time through the sequence.

Crosspicking #2: Reverse Roll, Alternate Picking

This exercise uses a four-note pattern, often called a *forward-reverse roll*. The even number of notes in the pattern lends itself well to alternate picking.

Crosspicking #3: Forward-Reverse Roll, Alternate Picking

The next two exercises are crosspicking examples that do not use alternate picking. This approach, often called *economy picking*, seeks to minimize awkward picking and string crossings through economy of motion. Notice that the pick direction in both examples changes to facilitate moving the right hand across the strings.

Crosspicking #4: Forward Roll, Economy Picking

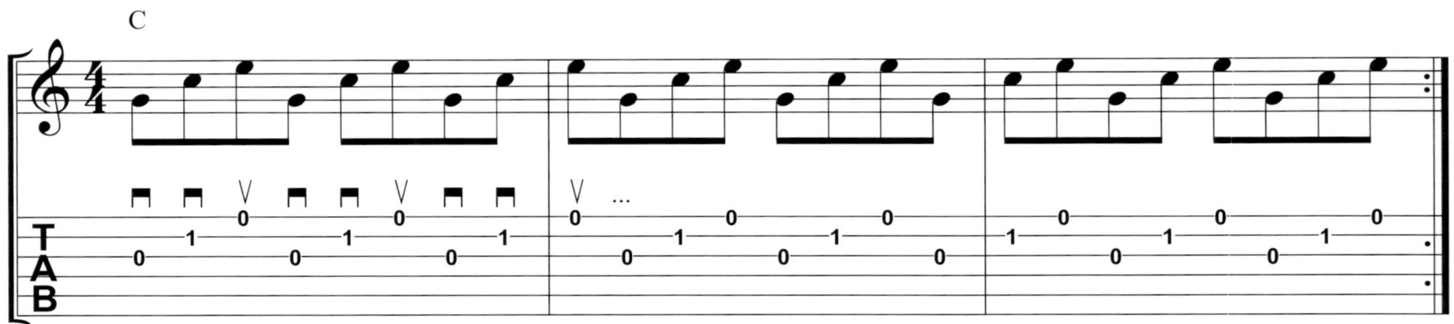

Crosspicking #5: Reverse Roll, Economy Picking

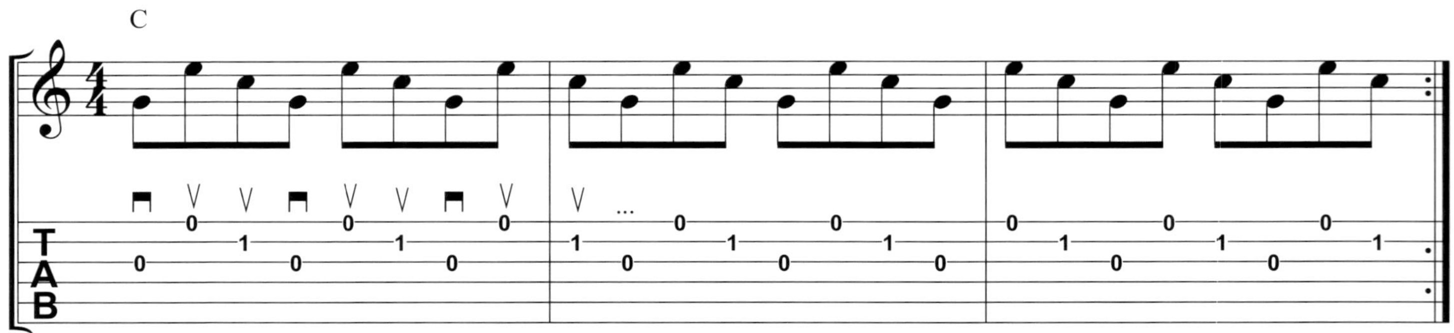

The different variations of rolls are often combined with one another. The following study combines forward rolls and forward-reverse rolls with a series of different chords. After learning this exercise using alternate picking as indicated, you may wish to experiment with economy picking techniques.

Crosspicking #6: Combining Rolls

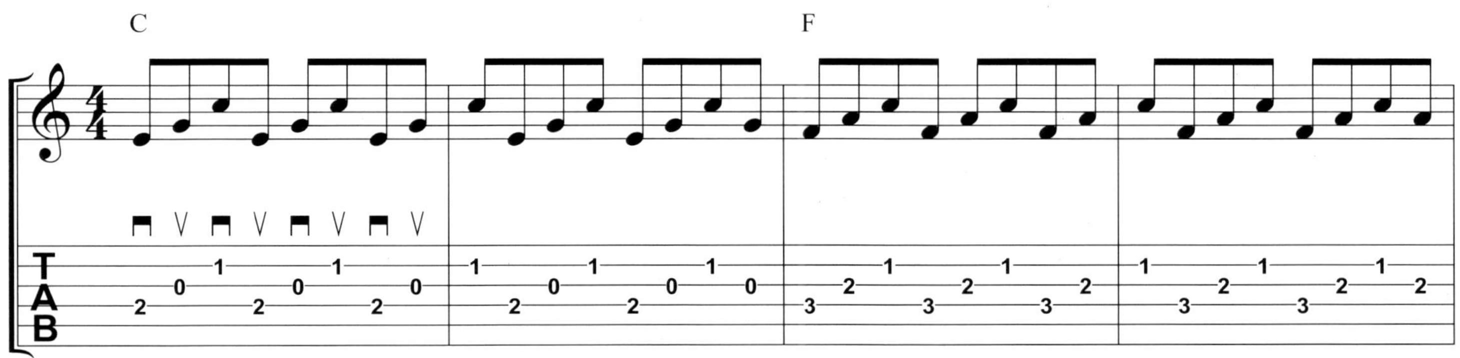

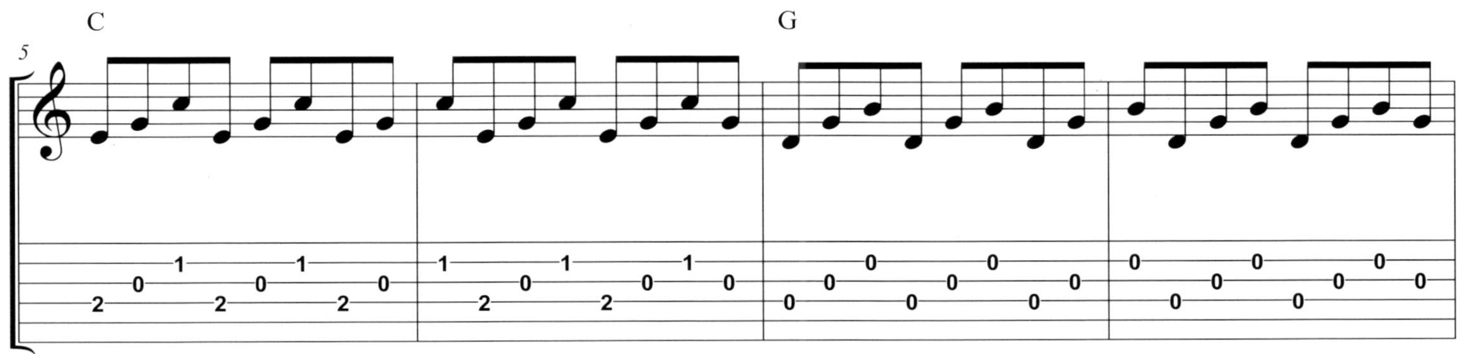

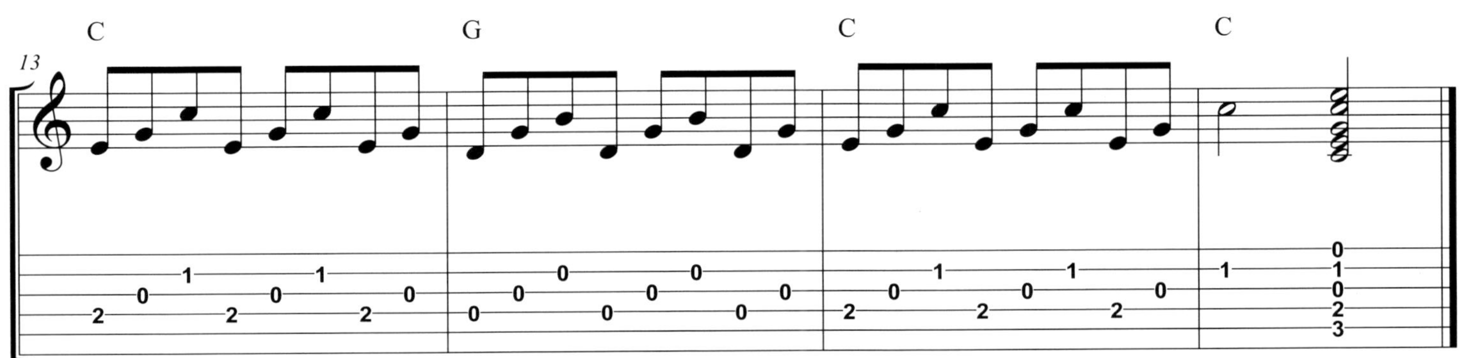

Once you are comfortable with the various crosspicking patterns, practice them over chord progressions from familiar songs. For example, the exercise below utilizes the chords from the song *Sittin' On Top of the World.*

Crosspicking #7:

Sittin' On Top of the World

Traditional

G G7

TAB

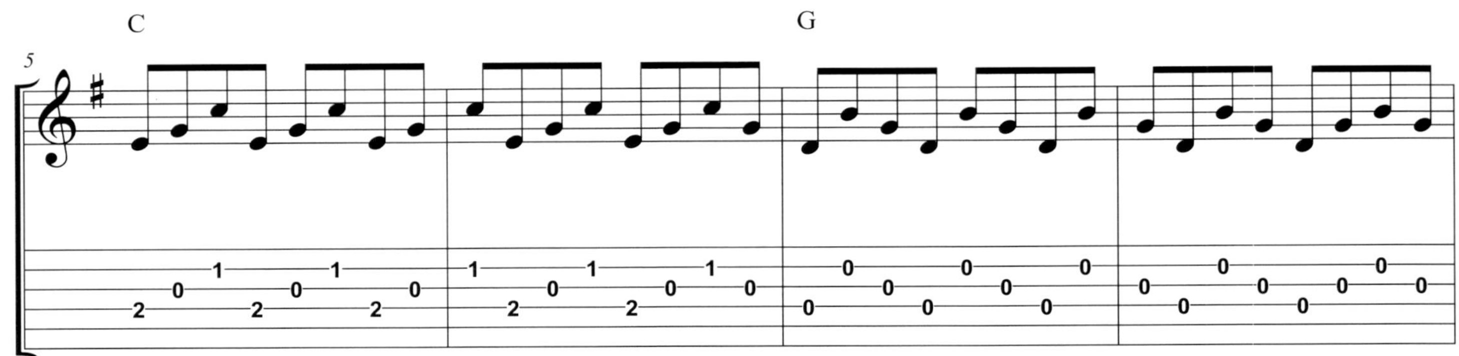

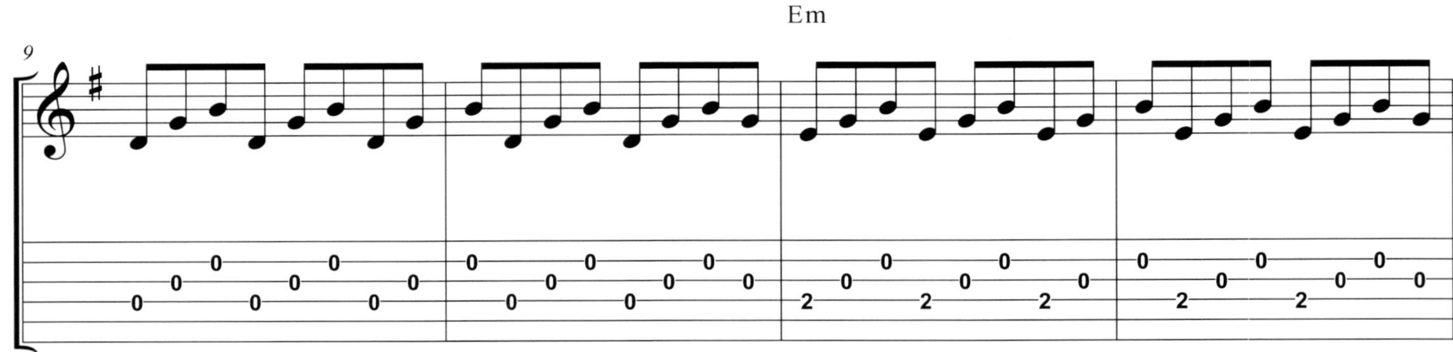

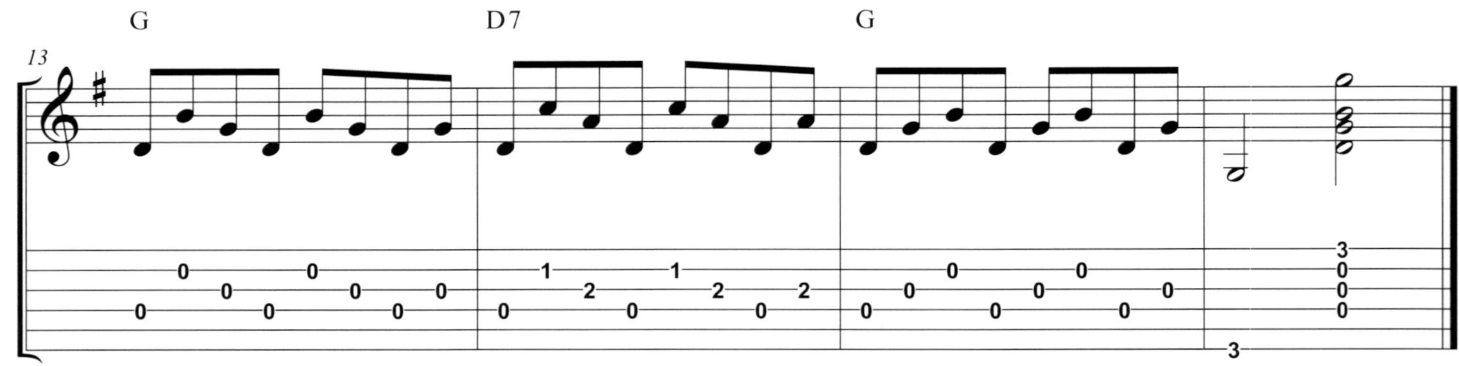

Try applying the crosspicking techniques you have learned by playing this tune.

Crosspicking #8:

Rest My Weary Head

Colin Botts

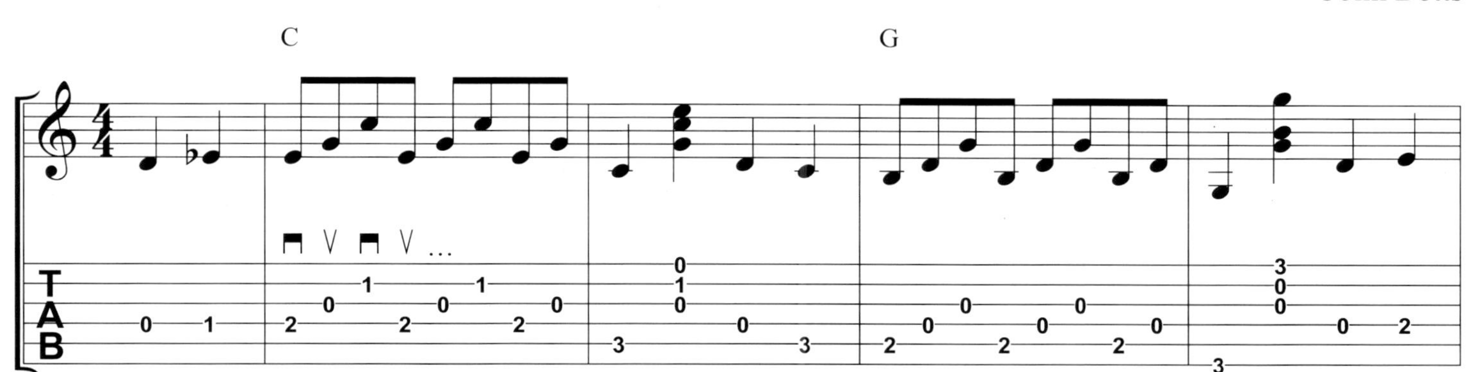

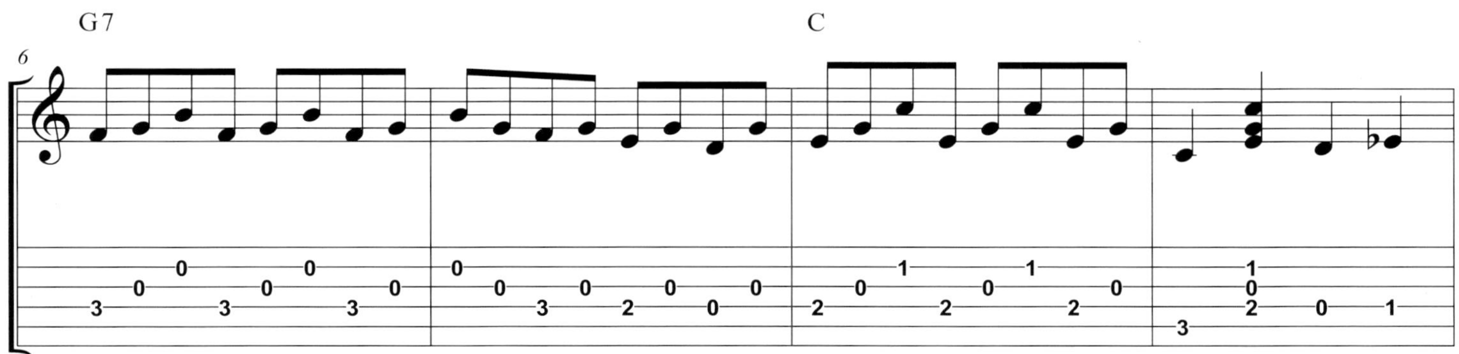

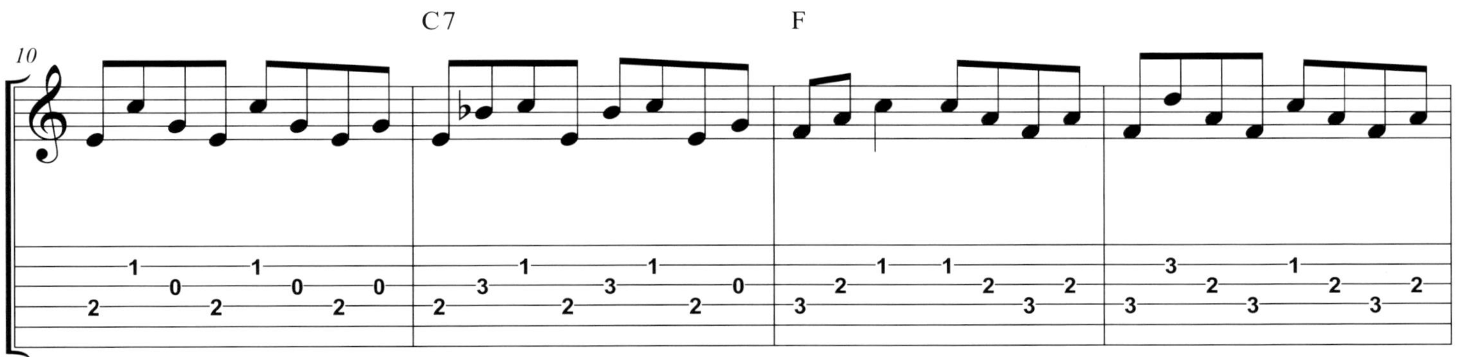

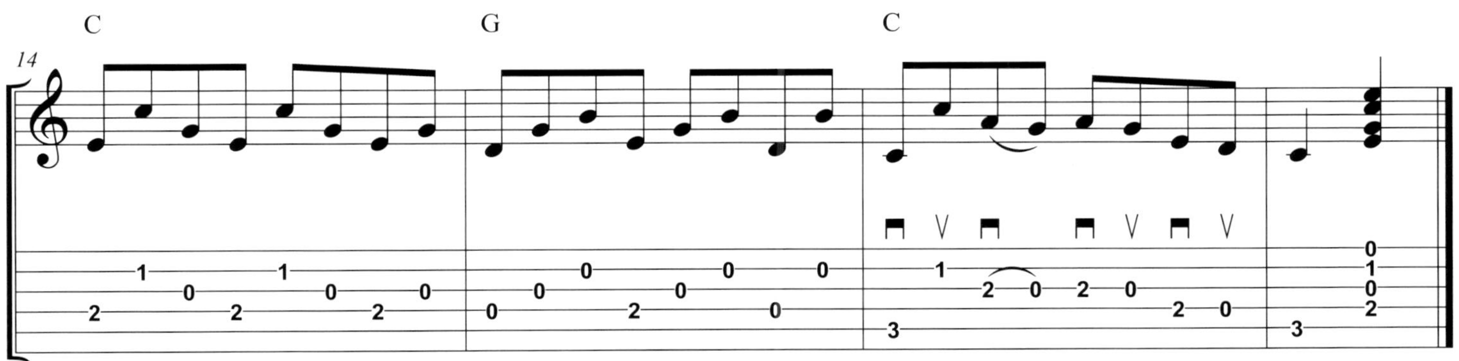

Once you feel that you have a good grasp of the crosspicking technique you might try incorporating melodies into your roll patterns. Keeping track of the melody while maintaining fluid rolls over the chord progression can prove a fun technical challenge. Practice the example below and then try coming up with some of your own.

Crosspicking #9:

Wildwood Flower

Traditional
arr. Botts

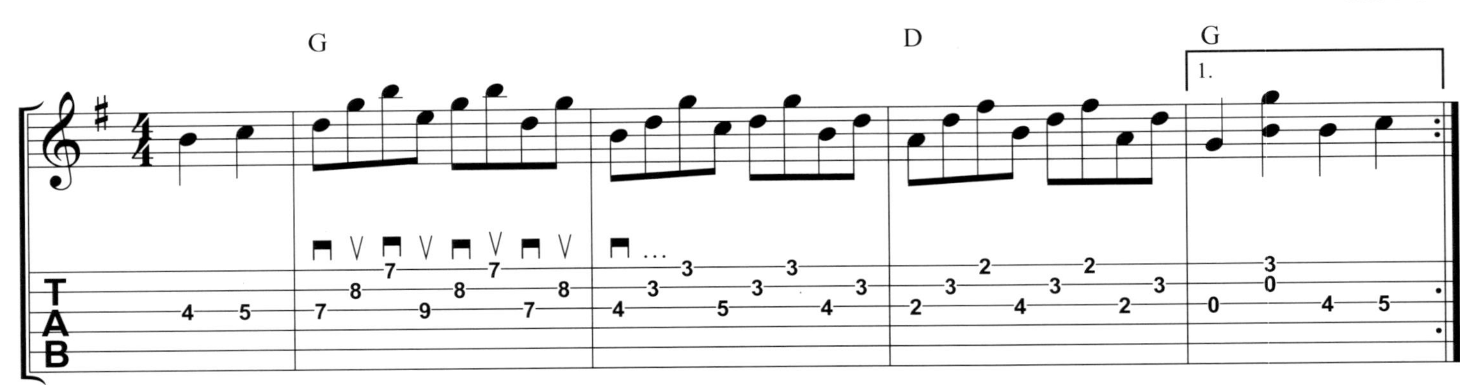

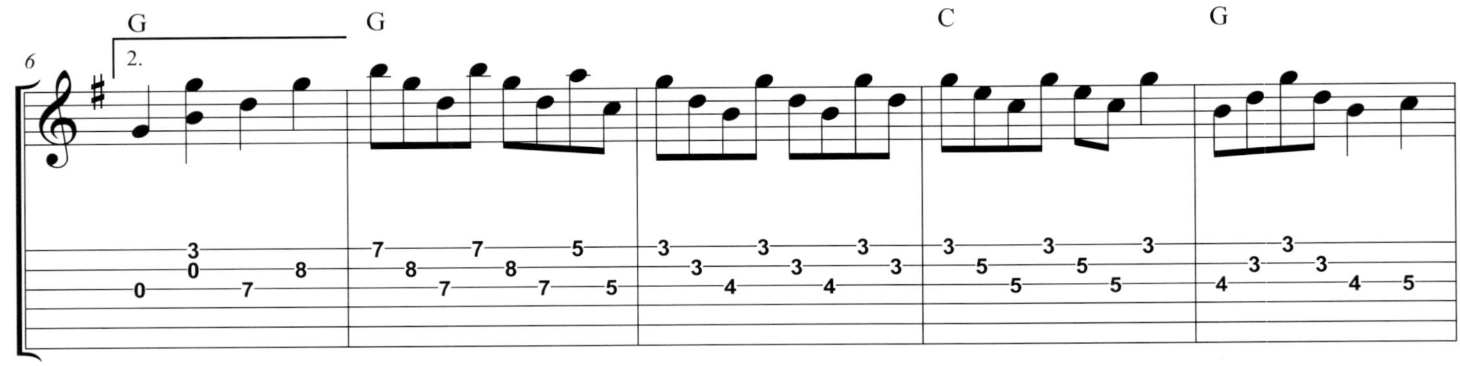

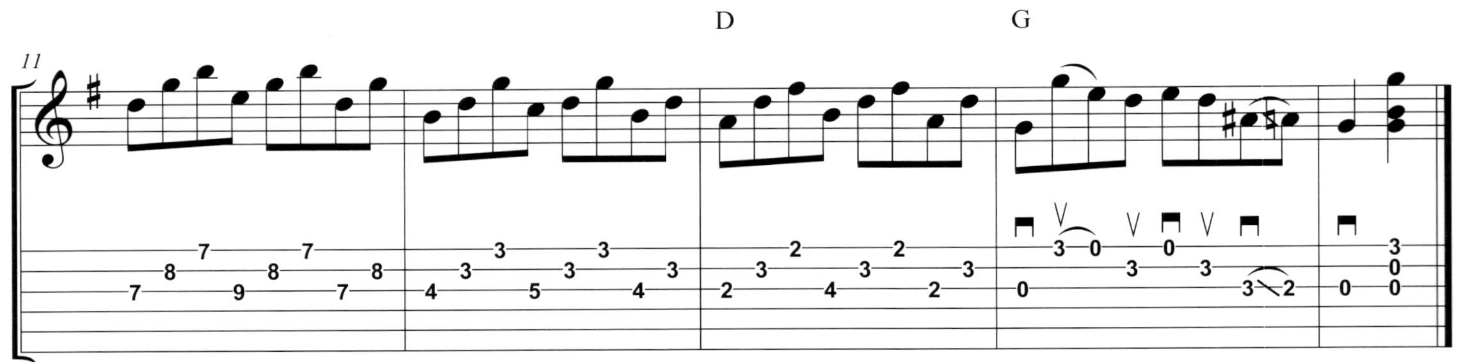

The final two crosspicking exercises combine various picking patterns with other techniques, including open string shifting and scale sequences. Have fun!

Crosspicking #10:

Charlotte Rag

Colin Botts

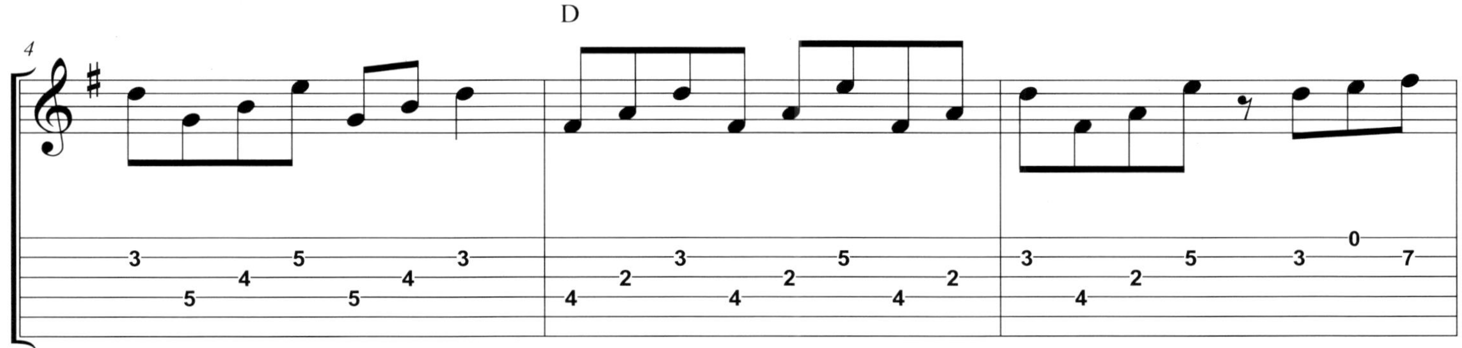

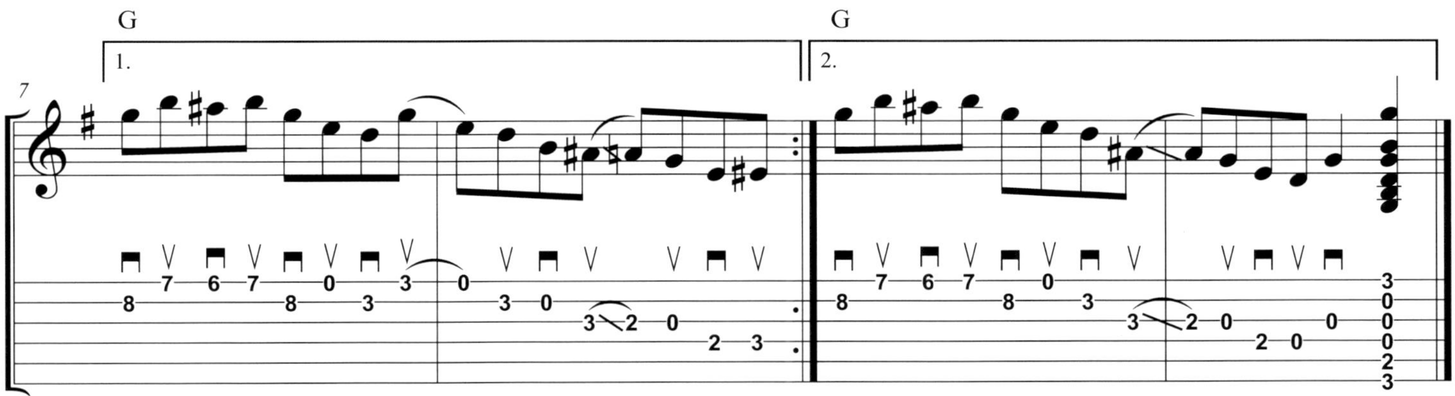

Crosspicking #11:

Dogwood Blues

Colin Botts

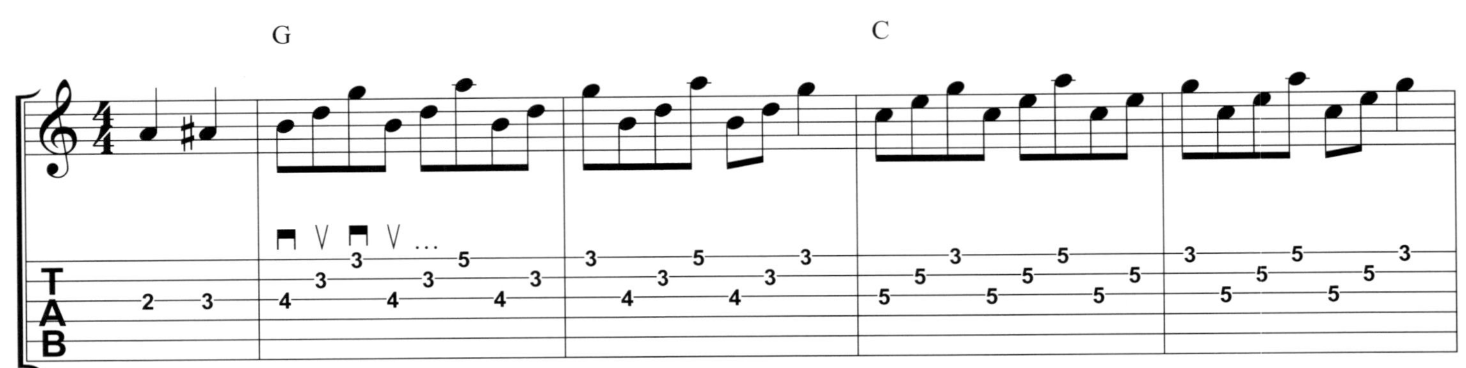

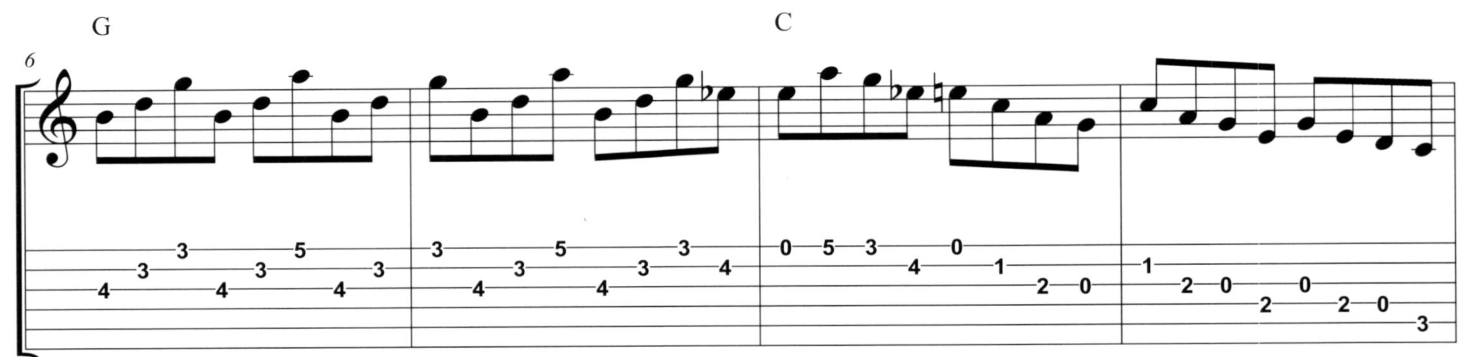

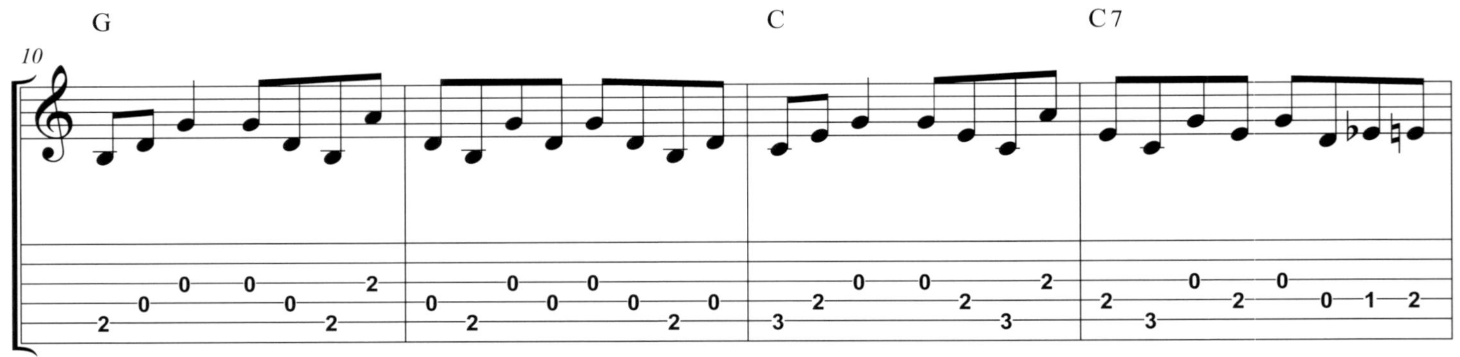

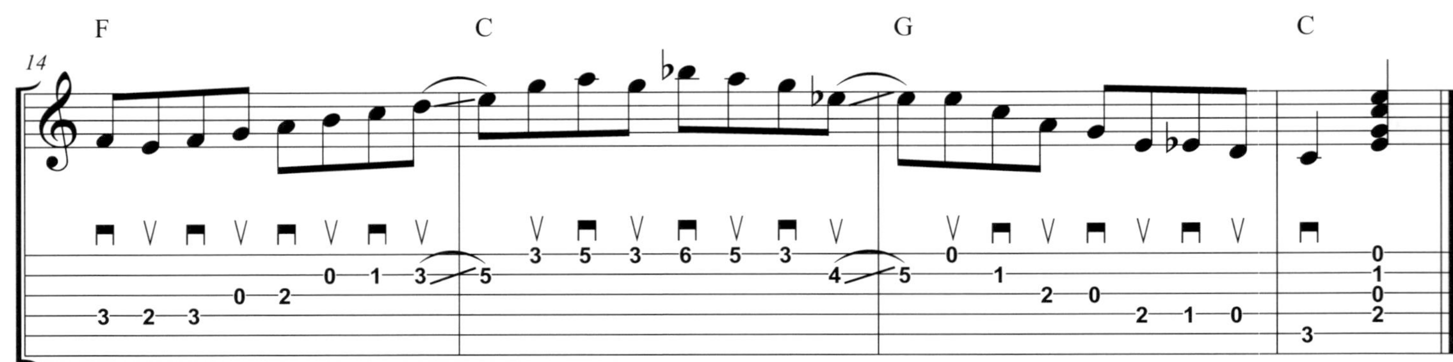

About the Authors

Colin Botts

As an accomplished multi-instrumentalist and former Capitol Records-Nashville recording artist, Colin Botts has performed on television, radio, and in hundreds of venues, both across the United States and internationally.

Music has taken Colin Botts around the world, having studied guitar from gauchos in Argentina, concertina and bouzouki from traditional musicians in Ireland, and fiddle from gypsies while traveling through Romania. In 2013 Colin was awarded a masters degree in Irish Traditional Music Performance from The University of Limerick, Ireland.

Colin Botts is a passionate and dedicated teacher with a degree in guitar education from Utah State University. He has had the privilege to teach and lecture in a variety of settings, from university classrooms to private lessons, as well as music camps and festivals.

Corey Christiansen

Corey is becoming recognized as one of the preeminent jazz guitarists in the world. A recording artist, writer, educator and performer, he has played and taught in literally every type of situation around the globe for the last decade. "Awakening," Corey's first CD as a leader, was the initial release on Mel Bay Records in 2004 and received critical acclaim throughout the jazz community. *MB3: Jazz Hits Vol. 1* marked a great leap in his national and international visibility as a player and producer. *Jazz Hits Vol. 1* spent three weeks as the No. 1 jazz recording on North American jazz radio. His first performance DVD – "Vic Juris & Corey Christiansen: Live at the Smithsonian Jazz Café" – was released in July 2006. Jazzwise-reviewer Mike Flynn gave the recording four stars, noting that "...Christiansen is well versed in the guitar's sonic heritage and his judicious sense of phrasing finds him light-fingered even on the densest of changes and positively euphoric on his ballad work." Corey has written several method books for Mel Bay Publications as well as articles for many of the major guitar magazines and *Downbeat Magazine*. Corey currently teaches at Utah State University and the famed Jacobs School of Music at Indiana University. He is also an artist-in-residence at Atlanta Institute of Music (Atlanta, GA), and Broadway Music School (Denver, CO).

MEL BAY